Twists and Turns

In The Road

Stockton Todd Holden

Printed in the United States of America
First Printing, 2016

ISBN 978-0-9860911-1-7

Cairn of Quartz Publishing
315 East Broadway
Bel Air, MD 21014

Also by Stockton Todd Holden:
Son, You Turn A Good Phrase (www.createspace.com/5166256)

Book design, production, and editing
Patrick M. Wallis

One of the major sounding boards in compiling these books has been the stout-hearted and ever resourceful Keith Alan Holbrook. Keith has been a close and personal friend for many years and has never been at a loss for words when offering his perspective. Many times in the production of these books we have asked his opinion...as a friend, a well-read person, and for just having an all around creative mind. Without hesitation, each and every time the question was posed, his comment has always emphatically been the same, "THIS BOOK IS BULLSHIT!"

Dazed and somewhat perplexed, we leave it for you the reader to decide.

When confronted about the statement, Mr. Holbrook explained, "I didn't say the book was bullshit, I said the process of doing the book was bullshit. You know, I have about six copies of the book in my home. Three of them are keeping the dining room table level. As long as the table holds up, I will always find value in these books."

Twists and Turns

The following is an account of the 1958 crash on Rocks Road by the owner and driver of the Triumph TR3 shown on the front cover, Tom Stark.

It should be mentioned here and now that Mr. Stark was the same individual who drove the getaway car with the author during the infamous caper of putting a skunk in the Bel Air Main Street Theater, retold later in these pages.

Tomfoolery, indeed.

*   *   *

We were testing newly installed 'Rupert' aircraft-style seat belts, which most likely saved our lives as we twisted and turned at twice the speed limit. We were heading southbound on the wet, rainy pavement of Rocks Road when Todd yelled out as we careened across the bridge at the Camp WoMeTo intersection, clipping off a utility pole on the left side of the road, then slamming into a stone and dirt bank on the right side. We re-crossed the road once again and slammed into the left bank, going airborne and flipping upside down onto the trunks of two small trees.

We found ourselves hanging upside down over the rocky rapids of Deer Creek! The seatbelts held us firmly in place and saved our lives! Neither of us anticipated testing the seat belts like this, but we were sure glad they worked.

STH

We could only open one door on the driver's side, the gas cap behind our heads had flipped open and we were getting soaked in gasoline. The situation was further compromised by downed, live electric wires arcing in the wet roadway. I think Todd said, "We gotta get outta the car before the gas ignites!" We unlocked the belts and fell ten feet into the cold waters of Deer Creek, which was good to get the gasoline off of us.

Dazed, but unhurt, we started to climb up and back to the road and heard a loud warning from someone up the bank to watch out for live wires. A Maryland State Trooper by the name of Trooper Bernard Elwood Coleman had responded and arrived a short time after we had crashed, took accident-scene photographs and later wrote a report.

As Trooper Coleman asked questions, I told him that I really did not know how the accident happened because I drove that road often and knew the twists and turns. The trooper agreed that in responding, he too almost lost control on a curve. I recall that later, Trooper Coleman drove both of us home.

My 'dream car' was severely damaged front to back and all sides, but we walked away by the grace of God. My pride and joy, only six weeks old, was broken, but we were not. Todd's dad, Gwynne Holden, sold his TR3 in short order and my TR3 ended up back at Foreign Motors on Cathedral Street in Baltimore where it had been purchased and now was there to be rebuilt. I was called by the dealer two or three times to review the

work being done and finally after two long months, I
signed off on the repairs and took delivery of a 'good as
new' British roadster. In fact, it looked better than new.

Three more of our friends also rolled their sports
cars: Bucky Hartman and Bill Berrell in TR3s and Larry
Thornton in an MG. Thornton flipped his car on the big
and sharp curve in Leeswood with Freddie Calcutt riding
shotgun and wearing his Bel Air High School football
helmet. The car had come to rest on Freddie's head,
pinning him to the ground. We had to lift the side of the
car to drag him out. Larry was ejected, but relatively
unscathed.

The Triumphs would lose traction easily and without
warning, but we all were wild, crazy and pretty much
deranged drivers. I even managed to wreck my TR3 two
more times, but again by the grace of God, I survived.
The last wreck totaled the car and I sold it to a junk
yard for $400. I used the money later that year to buy
a ½ carat diamond engagement ring for the lady of my
dreams.

I realized that God did have a better plan for me,
which probably excluded owning or driving a sports car.

I'm happy to say that my wife, Elizabeth, and I
celebrated our 54th wedding anniversary this year. I still
recall leaving Great Bridge, Virginia, on that special day
driving a 1955 Chevy Bel Air, two-door hardtop three
years older than the TR3.

To this day, Todd has only ridden two times in a car with me driving. Both of those times he voluntarily wore a full-face motorcycle helmet and we never rode through Rocks State Park together again.

Tom Stark, as I recall these events.
June 2016, Towson, Maryland

Tom Stark, in 1958, with his prized Triumph TR3.
It was good while it lasted. Photo by the Author.

*   *   *

Photo on the cover by Maryland State Trooper Bernard Elwood Coleman. Todd Holden travels Rocks Road whenever he can, driving slowly and enjoying the ride.

The road of life twists and turns and no two directions are ever the same. Yet our lessons come from the journey, not the destination.

Don Williams, Jr.

To Explain...

For those of you who enjoyed my first book, welcome to the second installment of stories originally appearing in The Delta Star. I'd like to thank Ron and Mike Sommer for being so kind as to run my stories week after week. I'd also like to thank the readers of the column here and abroad and for kind words when I needed them.

There has been no attempt to update the columns... dates and times apply to when they were written. Some details were added, but mostly these stories have stood the test of time, at least that's what my editor tells me.

I'm excited with this collection and hope you enjoy it too. Read, relate, enjoy, dispute, disagree...anything goes...if you must use a book or two to level a table or chair, please, take the time to read through these stories and then, well...perhaps you can use a wood shim for the furniture and loan the book to a friend.

Todd Holden
'illegitimi non carborundum'

* * *

The author would like to acknowledge the Rustica Executive Board members, Mina Horn and Barbara Szymanski, for their editorial skills, opinions and perspectives, as well as their valiant and untiring contributions not only to the success of this book, but for keeping the relative sanity of the author intact.

Look What The Dog Let In

R ustica has been my home for a long time. I make the rules and do pretty much as I want. There was a time I considered myself the Lord of the Castle, so to speak. But truth be known, Dude and Frisco are the real royalty of the house and run the show. My pal even calls them Lord Nelson and Lady Frisco. I have obediently become their caregiver and faithful servant here at the homestead.

Over the years, my pup Frisco, who will be eleven this Thanksgiving, has evolved into the matriarch of the home. When I come home she sniffs me out, checking where I've been and if I've been with any other animals, namely female pups. She convinces herself with that cold nose that all is good, and I let her out to run and romp. Sometimes I get involved with the computer or music and figure she's outside doing her thing, she's a dog, so I just let her stay out....

Lately when I let her out, The Dude goes out with her. He's four and many times follows her lead. Other times he does his own thing...like killing a groundhog. The two of them can completely dismantle a stone wall in less than an hour that I put together over several hours. They're also prone to walking the perimeter...surveying the land to see what mischief they can get into.

Sometimes Frisco gets a little impatient to come in and she's learned to open the sliding screen on the sunspace, which in cooler weather allows air to circulate through both floors. Every now and then Frisco appears, and I haven't let her in. Pretty amazing. She lets herself in, but hasn't figured out how to close the screen. Not wanting bugs or creatures slipping in unannounced I go to the screen as soon as I see her and close it.

Once I'm ensconced in the LazyBoy and the television is on the pups will come over and sniff my leg or nuzzle my foot...just doing what pups do. Such was the case the other night when I came home from a "Pimm's Party" up near Highland. The weather was perfect and I let the pups out, came back inside and turned on the music.

Getting a glass of water to help dilute the Pimms I reclined and relaxed. Next thing I know Frisco and Dude are licking my left leg and sniffing my foot. Normal...and to be honest I'd forgotten about how they got in.

A little later they were fast asleep on the tile floor of the kitchen, where it's really cool to be. I must have fallen asleep as well, because I woke up to what I thought was a cold nose on my ankle. Really cold nose I thought.

Never thought of the three recent black snake arrivals I'd accepted from folks who don't want them around their own place. Matter of fact all of them were set loose in the tool shed, adjacent to the house, where they could

forage in the cool darkness...or leave for other parts of the place...no matter to me...they are welcome guests... outside.

Imagine my surprise when I glanced over to the kitchen and saw Dude and Frisco still asleep. What was the 'cold nose on my ankle' pray tell.

Slowly lifting my head, I looked down and saw the 'cold nose'...seems the five foot black snake had also come through the open screen and wriggled his way over to the living room. He was stretched out on the carpet and I didn't want to alert the pups, so carefully I picked up the black and took him outside so he could get under the deck or amongst the spider flowers (Cleome).

All's well that ends well and I dimmed the lamp next to the recliner, made sure the doors were shut, and got the pups a little water. Just another day and evening at Rustica. We all get along very well, thank you.

========= 30 =========

Who Can It Be Now?

I ndulging myself a little pleasure, my iPod brings me music all the time, wherever I go. I don't listen to it when I'm walking outside much, although I suppose I could. I do bring it with me when I've got a doctor's appointment and sign in and settle in a chair for the customary long wait. Sometimes, on rainy days, I'll go walking in the mall and if I'm more in the mood to walk than chat with fellow 'mallers,' I'll just plug in and go.

By far, the best time for my iPod is when I slip it into its cradle in the Expedition and set off for a cruise to visit pals or just go. More on that later.

Years ago, in the nifty Volkswagen bus we used to travel in, for the long cruises with kids and pals there was an 8-track tape player and four 8-inch speakers plastered behind the front bucket seats and along the sides.

Oh my, how we rocked out on our way to Herb and Shela McComsey's mountain in Cornstalk, West Virginia. Each of us had our favorite tape to play along the way. Mina pushed in John Denver's 'Rocky Mountain High' and 'Greatest Hits'...Sam and I favored David Bowie's 'Space Oddity' and 'Major Tom' and all of Jim Croce's songs, while Ann insisted on Bruce Springsteen's 'Born To Run.'

Music made the trips even more fun than they were already. We literally wore some of those 8-track tapes out on the many trips we took in that cream and tan VW bus. Everywhere we went the first thing we did was fasten the seat belts, make sure everyone had made a pit stop, and then put in the tape.

A few of the 8-tracks that accompanied our trips and made it through the years. Photo by Sam Holden.

Our adventures with the 8-track tapes was a good tradition and one we never knew would take the steps into the future that it has, with cassettes, CDs and Sirius FM and the iPod. The music reaches most of us, and those of us who don't really care, well, we still listen and sometimes even ask to 'turn up the volume.'

If more folks just listened to music when they drove around, and stayed off the cell phones and texting their friends, maybe, just maybe the roads would be a lot safer...matter of fact, the roads no doubt would be safer if folks simple paid more attention to driving those deadly weapons we call cars and trucks.

There are so many distractions to interfere with our concentration when we're behind the wheel. Traffic is insanely heavy and dangerous, many of the major roads are seemingly always in some stage of construction or rehabilitation, and the workaholics weave in and out of the lanes of traffic like the Indy 500 was their game.

It seems odd that something as serious as the privilege of driving a vehicle has to be burdened with things that take our minds and eyes away from the road with oncoming traffic and panic stops.

Folks die every day in senseless accidents that no doubt were caused by inattention on the part of a driver. Foul weather, rain and snow, sleet and ice, all cause lots of accidents when we are alert and paying attention. So why do we risk a tragic mistake driving? Why add more drama to an already serious, dangerous activity when we drive on crowded highways and scenic back-country roads.

Just look out for the other guy, listen to the music, and leave the cell phone on the seat. Hey, when you are stopped at a light or getting a cup of coffee, you have all the time and safety in the world to check and make calls to the ones you missed when you were driving.

Think back to what it was like before cell phones... we all survived, we stopped and made calls from pay phones. Well certainly, the world has changed big time from when I was a young buck. We're told the world spins much faster these days, but even in a fast-paced world, we owe it to ourselves and the others on the road roaring past us to wait for the next stop to use the cell phone.

So do what I do. Dress properly, make your mandatory pit stop, and bring along some music. Remember, you don't have to turn it all the way up or install some mammoth creation that'll blow the siding off the house as you fly by. Pick your songs and enjoy the ride.

If you feel so inclined, don't be afraid to sing along. Just pay attention to the road, all that's happening, and let the world go by. Wasn't that an old tune by Eddy Arnold? No, I remember...in life as in music, sometimes we just want 'to make the world go away.'

========= 30 =========

Bootie's Still In Town

O h you can call
him Warrenell,
or you may call him
Boom Boom. You can
call him the Maryland
State Heavyweight
Champion (1959, beating
Burt Whitehurst in 12
bone-crushing rounds).
You can call him the All
Army Champion and toss
in the All Inner Services
Heavyweight Champion
as well.

Warrenell Lester, at his home on Shucks Road, 2003. Photo by Todd Holden.

Me? I just call him
Bootie, like I have since
I first met him back in the 50s in Bel Air, where he was
steadily making a name for himself and turning locals
on to boxing. He was our own pride and joy and he
fought by the name of Warrenell 'Boom Boom' Lester.
My last boxing memory of Bootie was the back of his
head hitting the deck at the Baltimore Coliseum after
Wayne Bethea clocked him with a right near the end of a
fight that Bootie had won on 9 rounds. I thought Bethea
had killed him.

Ernie Knox fought Bethea following the Lester
fight. Bethea won that fight too. He hit Knox with
such devastation that it put him into a coma and he

died shortly thereafter. This fight game is for real and yet, even today, it is riddled with corruption and good fighters who get lost in the shuffle as 'stepping stones' to big name fighters who are groomed by syndicates controlling every aspect of the game, according to Bootie.

Bootie continued his professional career in the ring, but that night our local hero lay horizontal to the canvas. When I sat and talked with Bootie in the late spring of 2003, he was 72, fit and trim, soft spoken and other than a nasal twang in his voice from years of taking punches, he showed none of the physical and mental wear and tear that mark so many fighters who stay in the ring too long. He told me he once took six deadly punches just so he could land that killer right.

When he was inducted into the Maryland Boxing Hall of Fame in 1981, a lavish feast was set before the members and inductees. Along with Bootie, Earl Mathias, Vince Bagli, Earl Clemons, Mickey O'Donnell and several others were to be honored for their respective accomplishments. For all the fanfare, the evening should have been a highlight for the Havre de Grace native.

"Hey. I only use a knife, fork and spoon to eat. They had more silverware on the table than I knew what to do with. A fork for this, a fork for that, two knives, lots of spoons. How do you eat chicken with a knife and a fork?"

One of Bootie's last fights was in 1959 when he
knocked out Terry Moore in the 5th round at the
Coliseum on Monroe Street in Baltimore. Later, Moore
would be struck by a car and die of the injuries, Bootie
recalls. "I spoke at his funeral. When I fought him he
had 'blown up' and was out of shape, but he still wanted
to fight me."

The memories from the Moore fight brought tears to
his eyes as he sat at the Hall of Fame fete. His last fight
as a pro was against Harold Carter at the Coliseum on
December 5, 1960.

"All my fights were tough, but I believe the amateur
fights were the toughest. Harder than the pros. You can
pace yourself in the pros, but in the amateurs you only
have three rounds to get the job done. Still, looking back
I enjoyed the amateur fights. They were pure and clean
and hard fought tests."

Born on January 17, 1931, in Havre de Grace, Bootie's
family moved to Bel Air in 1939. Paul and Olivia
Lester had three other children; Paul J. Jr., Harietta and
Catherine. Warrenell was named after a friend of his
dad's who came from Germany.

A life-changing scuffle, after the family settled in
the county seat, brought out an athletic skill young
Lester possessed. A bully by the name of Sonny Boy
Jackson punched Bootie in the mouth and made him
cry. Embarrassed, the 13-year-old Lester vowed to learn

to defend himself. A very similar 'bully' episode led both Heavyweight Champions Muhammed Ali and Mike Tyson to a fighting career.

From his River City days, he knew of Joe Bernardi and the Atomic AC. "I owe everything to Joe, he taught me how to handle myself. Not to get mad or angry. To fight clean, to be a man. I never forgot what that man taught me," Bootie said.

"When Sonny Boy hit me, I got up and told him, 'One day you'll meet your match' and while he laughed at me, I added, 'And it just might be me.' The laughing hurt me more than the punch did. The next time Sonny Boy hit me, I hit him back and he couldn't believe it. From then on, I was hooked on boxing. I trained long and hard."

"One day I was hitting the big bag, 'rat-atat-tat,' and Joe comes over and calls me Boom Boom. He said when I hit the bag with my right, that's what it sounded like."

He became a regular on the Baltimore-Havre de Grace boxing circuit. In 1952, he entered the Army where he was assigned to Special Services and the boxing team. He won the light-heavyweight and heavyweight Golden Gloves championships in Washington, D.C., the 2nd Army title, and then defeated Zora Foley for the All Army Crown. In the end he won the Inner Services Crown, defeating Navy, Air Force and Marine contenders.

"The Navy champ, Charlie Butler put up a good fight, and the Air Force Champ, he just gave up. The Marine boy, I tore his tail up too. Whipped them all."

He won 112 amateur fights, losing only 5, before turning professional on October 25, 1954, at the Coliseum whooping Claude Flagler, bringing the contest to a halt in the second round. Bootie went on to fight in 32 more professional bouts, fighting heavyweights and light-heavyweights. His best fighting weight was 180 pounds, packed on his 5-foot, 11-inch frame.

A fight many countians may recall was held at the Bel Air Racetrack in front of the clubhouse. Bootie defeated Larry Zernitz in front of the hometown crowd. In his corner was his longtime friend and trainer Pete Bass. Pete's brother Kenny was his manager. "I never lost a fight with Pete in my corner," he recalled. "The syndicate wanted their people in my corner. When I fought Bethea, they pushed Pete aside and put their man in. That's just the way it was."

"The greatest fight I ever saw was between Joey Maxim and Sugar Ray Robinson. No question about it." Bootie sparred with Archie Moore, who was preparing for the bloodletting that Rocky Marciano administered in a title fight in 1955. "Archie was my favorite fighter. It was a great break to live and train with him. He taught me not to telegraph my punches. Because of being in his camp I got to fight on the same card that night in Yankee Stadium against Wadell Hanna. I won and Archie lost."

Bootie didn't think Cassius Clay was all that good when he started. "He was groomed to be The Greatest. He had the 'stepping stones' to tread across on his way to the top."

"I didn't really care for Sonny Liston, but he sure was strong. Heck man, he had muscles in his eyebrows. Sugar Ray Robinson refused to give me an autograph after a Baltimore fight. That really hurt me. He could have done that, I was right there. But he didn't."

"Every fight I had in Baltimore, Quincy Edwards made sure I had a big Mercury Park Lane to drive up in. I never bought one though. I was a Buick man, and got my cars from Joe Lee. Yeah. A big green Buick convertible. Times were good."

"I was small, but I could take a punch. In Florida I fought Bob Satterfield and had him whipped. Then he hit me with a 'sacrifice punch', a punch that is all or nothing, and it landed, POW, and I went down. Everyone in the place knew the fight was over except me, cause I kept getting up. Hey man, Satterfield was the No. 1 ranked contender."

"Before I could fight him again he'd left the country to fight overseas. I couldn't get a return match until he came back, and he couldn't fight anyone else in the states until he fought me. He never did fight here again."

STH

I spent time with Bootie in early 2003, gathering notes for this story. Times were less frantic and violent for Bootie and his wife of forty-one years, Booby, the former Thelma Beatrice Banks. "We went steady for nine years, just to make sure. Bootie and Booby share stories of the fight game...the fame, fortunes and tragedies...each countering with facts from the past. At the time this story was written they were both working at Aberdeen Proving Ground.

Bootie died on June 5, 2004, of complications from cancer. He was 73. His life was cut short, but his legacy continues. He is survived by his wife, who has always loved her champion.

"Lots of good fighters die broke or broken or both. Tommy Morrison, Sugar Ray Robinson and Beau Jack. Beau was shining shoes when he died. The exceptions to the rule are Floyd Patterson and Archie Moore. They were protected. But the sad cases far outweigh the good. They really should have a funeral for the fight game today, compared to what it used to be," Bootie emphasizes.

Although they had no children, Bootie always lived by the "TTCTT" rule. "Tell The Children The Truth. Whatever you do, get the truth out."

That magical day back in the late spring of 2003, for a couple of hours in his home on Schucks Road, Bootie got 'the truth' out. I was spellbound listening to this hero of the ring who I had seen take punches and deliver them.

It was far more than I could deal with concerning the fight game and the way it goes. He hadn't 'made it' to the top and he filled out his years working a blue collar job with a smile on his face. He was never bitter because he just liked to fight. Money was not his goal. Maybe that's why he preferred the amateur days when things were plain and simple and true.

The author gives Bootie a run for his money in 2003. Photo by Booby Lester.

========= 30 =========

Todd Holden watched his first professional fights on television with his dad and brother. Wednesday night fights sponsored by Pabst Blue Ribbon beer. And the Friday night bouts from Saint Nick's Arena in New York. His favorite fighter was a mushroom farmer, Carmine Basillio, who could take punches all night long, lose, but never go down.

Bel Air and Delta
Characters Pass On

Many of you may have ventured into Bel Air on a weekend to shop or hang out in a local bar. If by chance you did partake of the eateries and bars, you might just have happened upon this one. It closed a few years ago, because of the failing health of the owner/barkeep. It's now a coffee shop, but in its day it was a spot where you could run into horse trainers from Country Life Farms, or a builder, brick mason, or even a journalist...or maybe just average farmers who had come to town to spend some of the milk check on clothes at the Hub or Hirsch's Men's Store and perhaps while the wife and kids were catching a malted at Woolworth's or Richardson's Drug store, you may have crossed then two-way Main street and ducked into the Kandy Kitchen.

Last week marked the passing of yet another icon of old school, the much beloved Peter N. Panos. The heart and soul of Bel Air's Main Street for many years, Pete passed away Monday, 25 March, and the main thoroughfare through Bel Air became just a little emptier.

You won't see the name of Pete Panos on any buildings or hear him honored for being a big noise. On the contrary, Pete, his brother Gus and his mom, Pota, were quiet, hard-working, middle-class folks with a passion for honest trading, human kindness and integrity. They ran a little store-front grille on Main

Street for many years called the Kandy Kitchen. It wasn't fancy, but it was comfortable with a bar and little wooden booths along one side of the narrow building.

Pete had a few helpers now and then, but he was there pretty much all of the time, except on bowling league days, when he opened after rolling a couple strikes...that's what made the place so neat. There were no signs on the door and if the t.v. was on, the place was open.

The Kandy Kitchen was my respite for many a visit, mainly because of the camaraderie. Folks showing respect and enjoying each other's company.

One night a bunch of rowdies rolled out of the Red Fox and started to cross the street. Pete was at the grille and he quickly locked the door and yelled down the bar, 'Turn off the t.v." The crowd got to the door and everyone in the place either froze or ducked down.

After some banging and cussing, they eventually left and the Oriole's game was back on the t.v. and things returned to normal.

Many times I was asked to lock the door or take someone home who had way too much to drink and I was glad to do it...for the wayward drinker, for Pete, and well, it's just what was done in those days.

The Kandy Kitchen was an institution totally under the radar. The late George L. Van Bibber took me there the first time when they had a freshly baked ham on the counter and you could cut the meat for a sandwich.

True, you likely won't see the Panos' name in the book of prominent Bel Airians and that's just fine. Yet, you will know of Pete, Pota and Gus in the souls of many of the hard-working, regular Joes who lived and worked in town and just wanted a friendly, quiet place to relax at the end of the day.

The end of the day came to Pete last week, and those who knew him and his little bar will never forget him. He's on a different Main Street now. We're fortunate to have had him on ours for a while.

========= 30 =========

The Latest Dude News...

Dude, patrolling his watch. Photo by Todd Holden.

A nyone who's ever had Jack Russell's knows they are fearless. Not to belabor my adventures with The Dude, my Jack Russell here at Rustica, the latest news is that he is okay and recuperating from a strenuous bout with a medium-sized female groundhog that was holed up in the tractor shed, behind and under a lot of lattices my son is storing there.

While my faithful mechanic pal Ron was working on my 25-year old Wheel Horse mower, with a stuck valve and a mouse nest in the coil, Dude and Frisco suddenly began barking in the shed. When a dog barks, I listen, because something is up, and they want me in on it.

By this time Ron has the head off the mower, has found and cleaned out the mouse nest, and is trying to 'unstick the valve' so I went to the shed and started moving the multitude of wood lattices. Dude was really getting into the pursuit. As he got closer I could tell both dogs were on to something, but I had no idea what. A rat? A squirrel? Chipmunk? Well, maybe a groundhog, since I had seen one digging on the outside of the shed.

As each sheet of lattice was turned over, Dude leaped at least 3 feet onto the back of a dark brown hog and the match was on. He has all his shots and he is a Jack... so this is supreme in his nature and one has to just let nature take its course. Besides, their holes and dens in the soybean field are not favorites of John Magness, who farms the place.

In brief, here is what happened...as I wrote to my son and a few pals who know Dude and follow his adventures...

"The dude was hurting last night, gave him 2 crushed up aspirin, mixed in w/yogurt...he loved it...he went to bed at 9...never stirred until dawn...

He was bitten several times on the shoulder and chest muscles...and the effects were felt at bed time...

This morning he is up and about...will rinse the wounds out again w/peroxide...only one small bite on his snout...

It was a fierce female groundhog that was cornered by Frisco and Dude...she put up a long, game fight...

She was unwelcome amongst us...

No shots were fired...and as per usual, my pups do not mutilate further after killing...

They are assassins, plain and simple...'they do the job, make certain of finality, and move on...'

Upon Release from the mansion master suite the morning after, he made for the pines for his morning constitutional...then returned to the scene of his latest and by far, greatest, triumph...Sam's lattice stash in the tractor shed where the groundhog met his match...

Dude is o.k....but needs a day of rest before the next bout...

Just keeping posted you who love and know the fearlessness of The Dudester..."

In this heat of summer, yesterday was a bit of excitement both for Ron and I...and the pups...sometimes it's true, 'there's never a dull moment around the place'... not always true, sometimes, but not all the time.

We don't look for trouble here at Rustica...we just try to protect and defend our little piece of land. We live in harmony with the creatures and nature, but then there are times...

By the way, Ron went to Coale's and bought a new head gasket, $14, fixed the valve, and put the engine back together. Mower runs fine...and with care might last longer than me. Life is good, and it needs the telling.

========= 30 =========

For the Love of Canoe Restoration

W hen I first heard that a pal was going to get in his Subaru and drive through a downpour, all the way to Burlington, Vermont, to pick up and haul back an antique wood-canvas canoe I wondered about his sanity.

What was unique is that this canoe just happened to have been built by the E. M. White Canoe Works in Old Town, Maine, in business from the early 1900's until the 1960's. This particular canoe dates around 1907 and was not in that bad a shape when Gordon Smith picked it up with his pal, Ray Schell.

Ray had learned of the canoe from an ad on eBay:

> "I have my great grandfather's canoe for sale. It was bought in New York City and bears a tag that reads "New York Sporting Goods Co. It was used on Lake Placid where my great-grandfather built a camp in 1905. It needs to be restored."

Going on this information Ray figured it was well worth the $300 asking price and he and Gordon decided it was worth a 'day trip' to pick it up. The canoe had

been stored in a garage for the past 30 years. In less than an hour the canoe was loaded on the roof-rack and the trip south began.

As snow started falling they headed back to Maryland where the canoe was going to be stored at Gordon's home in Bel Air.

Gordon Smith's next canoe project arrives in Bel Air.
Photo by Todd Holden.

Gordon has long been a member of the Chesapeake Wooden Boat Builders, based at the Havre de Grace Maritime Museum. He is a mentor in the eclectic group of wooden boat lovers who handle all manner of restoration and repairs through their membership.

Trust me, when you visit their headquarters in Havre de Grace less than a stone's throw from the ancient, white Concord Point lighthouse, you will be awakened to

the sights of all manner of water craft, in all stages of a sort of 'wooden autopsy.' Yes, the dismembered pieces of keel, gunnels, decks, thwarts, seats, planking and canvas make up the vital organs of a canoe.

Virtually each restoration begins with a total 'dissection' of the parts of each craft. This 'new' canoe will begin restoration in July with damaged and broken planking being removed and replaced with new wood. The old varnish is stripped out and the entire inside is re-varnished, making the canoe ready for new canvas.

After the canvas is applied it must be filled with a water-proof sealer, and hung up to dry for at least six weeks. After that the sanding begins and then final painting is done.

This entire process can take two to three months and since this is an E.M. White, the canoe will be tested on the water, paddled and stored at Gordon's home. The canoe was bought and paid for by Gordon, who also works on canoes at his home. You might say he has a consuming hobby when it comes to canoes. A labor of love if there ever was one.

The wooden boat builder's school is part of the curriculum at Harford Community College and is open to all ages. The group meets every Tuesday evening from 7 to 9:30 at the museum.

In his spare time, Gordon also takes care of much of the maintenance including mowing the grounds and miscellaneous repairs to the building.

When I stopped by that day before Gordon and Ray left town, I sensed the feeling of adventure in both of these two characters...a youthful enthusiasm if you will...of men who love making old boats new again. A visit to the museum and the various boats on display in various stages of restoration will give anyone a richer appreciation of wooden boats and their history.

========= 30 =========

The boat building class is now located in Cecil County in the town of Northeast. Still under the curriculum of Harford Community College.

Some Things Get Better Every Year

It's not the kids jumping in the pond, tossing each other in and dodging the occasional pine cone being tossed by others in a game of water dodge ball.

It's not the classic Camaro convertible sitting under the shade of a maple tree...pristine amidst all the laughter and camaraderie.

It's not the bounty of excellent food, brought as 'covered dishes' and all manner of picnic fare. It's not the long cooked pig, that's just been dug out of the coals, rich and steaming and fit for a king.

It's not the weather, which today is getting cooler as storm clouds approach but never dare to rain on this annual picnic in Whiteford.

Nah, it's none of the above singularly...it's the sum total of farm folks, with lots of common sense who manage to take care of themselves, not just today for the annual Les 'Caneman' Whiteford and his great wife, Janet's annual throw down picnic...but every single day of the year...these are heart-felt, good-natured folks, who share what they have and take care of those who come by to visit.

STH

Today it's another of the fine picnics for young and old, some from Tennessee, visiting relatives up 'north' and most of us, just 'home grown' native sons who wouldn't miss this event for the world.

Ross Blake welcomes me, as he always does at Slate Ridge oyster roasts...he's a good will ambassador of the highest degree and not a bit shy about providing a plate of food or a frosty, adult beverage. Seems it's this way with everyone in the pavilion.

Personally I never cared for catfish...my folks loved it, had it many times when they wintered in Florida...would go out of their way to get to a church sponsored 'fish fry'...yuck, on my end.

Until...until I was offered some of Bob Johnson's special battered catfish at Caneman's picnic several years ago. Bob persisted that I try some, to which I obliged, hesitantly to say the least. Oh my God...I have never tasted a seafood delicacy like Bob's Catfish...incredible... and I've been a fan ever since.

Plates of fresh roasted corn, homemade pasta salads, a bounty of food from all the folks who never come empty handed.

The kids swimming in the pond delight all and bring a smile to all those around. Harkens back to a time when we would hit the big pond at Southampton after putting

up hay or combining. Itching all over from the chafe we would strip and belly-flop in the spring fed pond as the sun was setting on another day on a dairy farm.

Les and Janet farm big time, and when the work is put aside for the day they party big time. They are the 'host and hostess with the mostest' when it comes to the June picnic. There's Robbie Martin running the Gator up and down the lane to the lawn parking area...Robbie is the 'taxi driver for the elderly' and the young and loaded as well and me, with the bum knee. After a day of eating and supping the climb back up the lane to the car is a bit of a challenge and a ride in the Gator is a fine ride indeed. Thanks Robbie.

A steady stream of grilled meat is coming off the heat all afternoon long...along with the pig and the tasty catfish. Helping create this fabulous feast are Greg and Kathy Harrison, Rich Tarbert and Jimmy Poole, and God knows who else, who just pitch in as needed...you don't need an invite to help pull onion rings and asparagus off the grille...just common sense, and there's plenty of that for this home-style cook out.

Folks sit and chat in the pavilion making new acquaintances and renewing old ones...catching up on all the news from those who we don't see often enough.

For me lots of the folks who make the Slate Ridge oyster roasts the hit that they are, are on hand doing the cooking at Caneman's. It's one big happy family of folks who like to see friends have fun and not go away hungry.

Les 'Caneman' Whiteford proudly displays a Todd Holden
photograph from last year's Whiteford's Picnic. Photo by Todd
Holden.

This is what the old days were like with church
picnics and other social events that have long since
passed into the orchestrated and regulated events we are
left with today. This is the way it used to be, with barn
raisings, square dances and being good neighbors.

There's the Harley-Davidson's parked all over the
hillside, along with pick-up trucks and SUVs...you can
tell the type of folks who are here, because in a snow
storm they'd be the ones pulling others out of the ditch.
I've never seen so many John Deere tractors and farm
implements as there are at Caneman's.

Today is the best ever...simply because it continues a tradition that surely must have begun years ago with a simple picnic for neighbors and friends...

If such is the case, Caneman and Janet have a multitude of friends and each of the 'friends' has more friends, and the cycle goes on. You can't go to the Whiteford's picnic and feel like a stranger...no way, buddy!

If you're invited and don't go, your loss...if you are invited, get some suds, cold sodas, and a homemade batch of potato salad and saddle up hoss, the wagons are circled and the dinner bell is ringing all day long.

God bless the folks all over who do the same as Caneman, this just happens to be the one for me every year. If you've got one to go to and catch up with all the friends, be getting to it while you can.

It's this link with the good times, and good spirit that we grew up with in Harford country that reassures me solid families are alive and well and carrying on long, established traditions.

On the ride home, a sprinkle of rain starts, much needed rain...and the warm feeling of being with friends surrounds me...Caneman, as ever in his dark blue Dickie overalls and the straw hat. I don't think I'd recognize him in any other outfit.

Waking up the morning after, for a moment as the
sun eases across the room falling on me and Dude
and Frisco...I feel all is well in this old world...a good,
reassuring feeling about life in general...the feeling is a
carryover from being in the best place ever, at the best
time...on the best day.

I'm sure many readers have similar events every year,
with friends and family and loved ones galore. How it
ever came to be I'll never know, but the 'Whiteford Way'
of saying, 'Stop on over, sit a spell, and dine with folks of
a like mind' just seems to hit the spot with me....

Hopefully you'll do the same this year as well...and
good for you...don't miss out on any family get-together
because it's like a tonic for the heart and soul.

========= 30 =========

Looking For Big Rock Candy Mountain

Burl Ives sang about it, even though he sugar coated the lyrics quite a bit. Goober Pyle didn't come from there, but he sure deserves to be working in the filling station somewhere near the peak. In medieval times, they called it the Land of Cockaigne where hardships didn't exist and the milk and honey flowed. The Big Rock Candy Mountain is where a lot of us grew up and learned our way of living.

The themes of early television series like *The Andy Griffith Show, Happy Days, The Honeymooners*...all beckon to the days of innocence and goodness. We remember the old days and seek to somehow reinvent the old ways, but they are plowed under by corporate greed, the trappings of modern life and the realization that you just can't go back all the way.

Goober wasn't a Yale Graduate, but he could take a car apart and put it back together in nothing flat. Ralph Kramden lost his cool a lot, but he had a soft heart, loved his wife, and was truly devoted to his pal, Ed Norton.

Today it's not the innocence any more...the land of plenty has turned selfish, conniving and ruthless to the average working Joe, who just wants to raise a family, have a week or two for vacation, and settle back and enjoy what's left of their life in retirement.

The daily news is not good for those of us who've worked our lives into retirement of sorts. Folks like Earl McIntyre, one of the finest mechanics ever to grace the area is retired, been retired for a while. He is old, older than me, and yet still heads out to his garage on Asbury Road south of Churchville to work on all manner of tractors, lawn mowers, the things we put gasoline into and hope they start when we have work to do.

Yes, Earl is getting up there, but he has to work at the little jobs for two reasons. One is the cash for sure, and the other is to keep on 'keeping on'...to keep busy, to continue to repair and fix up the broken things people bring to him.

Ask any farmer who is still in business and they'll tell you the cost of repairs, fuel, insurance all add up to big bills at the end of the year when it comes 'tax time.'

So the old timers help each other find that Big Rock Candy Mountain...it's just that a lot of time has passed in the interim. Roll back the clock forty or fifty years, and you'll see what I mean.

Back then, when the mower broke or some carpentry was needed, we called the folks we knew in the area who did that kind of work. Us and them, so to speak, we did 'trading'...we did 'business' with the people we knew who could do the job, do it right, charge a fair price and everyone came away happy.

Today, some of those folks are still around, like Earl, Bob Kennedy, Denny Ayres...and they are not all quite retired, but slowing down and picking the jobs they want to do, for folks who respect their talent and skill. They don't need the rat-race of today's way of doing business.

The folks who still take their jobs to these people, and some others like them know they will be treated fairly, and given sound advice. They know this because of the track record over the years. And when they pass on or are no longer able to do the work they loved to do, they are not usually replaced.

Sometimes a son or daughter will step in along the way and become part of the 'family' in the trade their family started. The torch is passed and we are blessed with another generation that carries on as they were taught by their elders. Happens that way in the car repair business and other trades. It's that way most times with dairy farming as well.

So it is that we go back to the pump and fill our cups with the ones who were fair to us. And the folks who tend our needs are grateful as well, that they are not forgotten or passed over. They are still vital in the area where they chose to be so many years ago.

It's a good feeling to call up Earl McIntyre and hear his voice; though he's mellowed with age and picked up some ailments, he's still the same chipper person we always knew. We ask if he still repairs mowers, and he says enthusiastically, "Yessir, sure do!"

We know our mower will be well taken care of and everything will work out. We're thankful we aren't given the run around by some nondescript merchant or a claim check with a number to check on sometime next week. We know this person and are grateful to have the service they offer.

Back in the day, we all lived on the Big Rock Candy Mountain. Life wasn't perfect like the song says, but it sure was a good way to be. It's an old time thing I reckon, but it's a good thing, and it's going fast.

========= 30 =========

Gene, It's Been Good To Know You

S ome folks we've known nearly all of our lives, some we've just met, yet feel like we've known them just as long...like a well-worn shirt they become part of the fabric of our own lives. When these folks depart from this world it leaves us wondering what made them so special to us and others.

Gene Miller was a special friend not only to me, but to just about anyone who had the good fortune to become acquainted with his gentle manner and warm smile.

Gene, enjoying the evening at Pop's Place in February 2012. The music was only part of the fun as Gene loved to tell stories that sometimes took weeks to finish. Yet, he knew every detail and every memory. Photo by Todd Holden.

I hadn't known Gene that long, and the first time I met him he gave me the once-over because he wasn't too sure what I was up to. You see, it was my first visit to Pop's Place, that farm with the barn where everyday folks come to play bluegrass music, sit and knit and share news of the week with one another. I sat with Gene many a night at Pop's place (Pop is William Hicks) and sat with Gene one afternoon to talk about his life and times.

My editor, Pat Wallis, plays the harmonica as Gene did and the two of them struck up their own special bond some time back. After Pat had a couple of heart attacks and a triple by-pass, I suggested he accompany me to Pop's in hopes of lifting his spirits. Pat felt right at home and it wasn't long before he and Gene were fixtures at the back table, playing along to whoever was up on stage.

We were both humbled and obligated to sit with Gene recently to talk of life, of Pop's, and how bluegrass music brought it all together.

Gene Miller, on right, plays harmonica with Pat Wallis at a Pop's Place bluegrass session in May 2012. Gene passed away on December 1, 2012, from complications of cancer. Photo by Todd Holden.

Totally under the radar of the fast-paced life around us, the folks who farmed, who worked on trucks and drove them rolled in to the Hicks farm, Pop's Place, weekly to dance, play and listen to music with friends and family.

Gene was born June 10, 1929, in a North Dakota farm house. There were three sets of twins, a sister and Gene. His parents gave him a harmonica when he was about 6 and he went through the house blowing in and out.

The way Gene tells it, he figured he had best learn to play it or else his parents just might take it away. The first song he learned was 'Jesus Loves Me' and it remained a favorite till the day he died.

Just before Thanksgiving, I sat with Gene and Dorothy in their kitchen on the Hicks farm. Pat came along to see his friend. Before any conversation was started, Gene was asked to play the harmonica for Scott and Arlyn, his son-in-law and daughter.

"Pat, let's try something in A." With pen in hand, I listened to the warm sound of the two harmonicas and took notes leading up to my interview with Gene. Dorothy chimed in, "Well, he also wakes up in the middle of the night when he can't sleep and I can hear him playing the harmonica."

Needless to say, harmonicas have always been a large part of Gene's life. So has singing, but more of that later.

The urgency to sit and talk with Gene was that he was dealing with very aggressive cancer now. "I'm trying to tough it out. The mass was shrinking, but now it's on the move again. At my age we prayed and opted out of chemotherapy."

Early on Gene worked construction jobs, ending up in Abingdon building a new post office there and the lady he would later marry, Dorothy Hicks was baking in Santoni's Market. Gene caught a whiff of her sugar cookies and soon met the love of his life. Dorothy's dad was William Hicks who was a big fan of bluegrass music.

Pop Hicks would travel to Bob Farrington's Mobile station on Route 1 in Hickory to listen to music on weekends. Popular with the locals, the venue eventually had to close down because of parking along the busy road. The music then moved to a coon club setting, then the V.F.W. near Poplar Grove, the fans following along.

Something closer to home was in his mind, and Pop was in his 80s when he set out to achieve 'an old man's dream'...much to the consternation of his close friends who doubted he could.

"I'm sorry, but that's an old man's dream that will never come true," Linda Stoval, a local clogger, commented at the time.

Pop began cleaning out his barn, putting in a concrete floor where there had been dirt, buying surplus doors to make paneling for the walls. He hoped to have a place where people could come and listen to local talent and enjoy the company of others.

From the beginning, Pop wanted some rules followed, such as no alcohol and no fighting. Good, wholesome music and good, wholesome people. Nothing wrong with that. These original rules are posted near the barn door for anyone to read and heed.

His dream was coming true, folks pitched in. Carmine Coleman, Bud and Paul Campbell, Bob Padget and others. They poured the concrete floor on a Tuesday, Dorothy recalls, "and by Friday evening we had music in the barn for the first time." It was October 1995, cold weather, a crock pot, some hot dogs and coffee, a chunk stove and an outhouse. Later, a kerosene heater, indoor bathrooms and interior decorating brought the place into shape.

From the day he met him, Gene was enthralled with Pop Hicks. Gene was in love with his daughter, but he quickly formed a close bond with his future father-in-law. He grew to love Pop and became an integral part of the family.

"He was an amazing man," Gene says, with tears of love and respect in his eyes. "I would drive him to listen to music all over the place, and now he could have music

on his farm." Friends donated their time, materials, and cash to provide amps, lighting and whatever else they saw that was needed.

Gene and Dorothy originally were not big fans of bluegrass, believe it or not. They went together 13 years and were happily married 15 years making it a 28-year love affair.

For many years, Gene sang with the Chorus of the Chesapeake and the Bay Country Gentlemen, two of the more prominent a capella male chorus groups. He also sang with many smaller barber shop groups and won many competitions.

With a song forever in his heart, Gene was never far away from his pitch pipe. Photo by Todd Holden.

The night after Thanksgiving this year he was able
to sing with the last quartet he was active with, The Old
Gray Hairs. "Yes, the old gray mare she ain't what she
used to be," he says. The group of friends and fellow
barber shoppers as they are called huddled in Gene's
room and sang, "Lida Rose" and "Let Me Call You
Sweetheart" with reckless abandon. Through the brief
visit Gene had with his old friends, they sang and shared
a story or two as Gene sat on the edge of his bed.

Gene was married twice before he married Dorothy.
His first wife, the mother of his four children has since
passed away. The interview was going deep at this
point, so I pressed on. "Now that you're coming to the
end of your life," I asked, "do you have any regrets?
"My one regret," he said without hesitation, "is that I
didn't tough it out with my first wife. I should have just
forgiven her, but I couldn't."

A little aside in our conversation, as is always the
case when you spend time with Gene. He mentioned
an article he had read in Reader's Digest many years
ago. The article talked of a survey about marriages
and why they failed. It seems the primary reason for
failed marriages was sexual problems. Second, money
problems, he recalled after all these years.

There was a third category Gene mentioned...that was
the 'miscellaneous and sundry' category. For many years
he didn't understand what that one meant and when he
and Dorothy married, he flat out told her he hoped he
never found out what that third one was.

As we talked this late fall day, he let me know he thinks he finally figured out what miscellaneous and sundry means..."it's the health or things that you have no control over."

The covenant built between Gene and Dorothy will surpass any survey in Readers Digest or any other magazine.

Another event he mentions is the day Pop died. It was June 10, 2001, Gene and Pop had planned on going to a bluegrass festival in Westminster, Maryland. Pop was not able to make the trip and died that day.

One of the last photographs of Gene, still the dapper gentleman. Here, he plays harmonica while Siebren Meulenberg plays the accordian. The tune...'Jesus Loves Me.' Photo by Todd Holden.

"I loved him with all my heart," Gene tearfully recalled.

In the time I've had the pleasure of his company, I feel like I've known Gene a thousand years and have the same sentiments for him as he had for Pop.

Time waits for no one and making the moments count adds up to precious times. So it was that Gene Miller showed us all a special time the minute he walked into our lives. With a warm, gracious smile and the soul of a troubadour, Gene is still teaching us all the special meaning of life and friendship, of good times and counting your blessings. He had the heart of a hundred men...it was good to know him.

========= 30 =========

Blue Lake

I've called her blue lake ever since the chromes came home from the lab and were laid out on a light table. On the roll were scenes of mountains, lakes, logging trucks and this one chrome...blew my mind and most everyone's who saw it afterwards. The photograph was one of a kind, at least for me. It was a shot to grace many homes and offices as the years rolled on.

The photograph was taken in British Columbia en route to Prince Rupert in October 1972. It was a road-trip with Will Pardew in his 1966 maroon Mustang.

My treasured *Blue Lake*. Photo by Todd Holden

My good friend Will was heading for the Queen
Charlotte Islands to work the salmon boats. I had just
quit the grind of the newspaper business and soon would
embark on a career as a professional photographer.

Will and my wife thought it would be good for me
to get away and a road-trip was suggested. At first I
was gung-ho but then got cold feet when the countdown
neared 7 days. How they ever got me in the beautiful
Mustang that fall morning I'll never know.

The pace of seven days a week covering crime, fires,
accidents and local government in Havre de Grace and
Bel Air had gotten to me. Now it was off my back, with
coffee and a buddy and the open road ahead of us. I had
dreamed of this kind of getaway but never had the guts
or gumption to do it. And if Will hadn't taken on with
the fishing boats the trip would never have happened.

He had traveled alone across the country. I had gone
on family trips to Maine and Florida and that was it.
Soon the names of towns stringing to the great northwest
would fill my mind and frames of film were captured at
a turning point in my life.

Des Moines, Cheyenne, Jackson Hole, Mount
Rushmore, Billings and Shelby, Montana drift by now in
memories of big trucks, open spaces, moose, cafes with
fresh coffee, taking time with car and open road. With
a good buddy who was going away for a salmon fishing
season, and maybe more.

Crossing into Canada through Chilliwack, then drifting northeastward to Kamloops, the drive was taking on a more surreal aura of newness and friendliness in new territory. It seemed so natural and easy to get in the car and drive to Prince Rupert, British Columbia, because that's where Will chose to work and if I wanted to ride along with him, kick back and do some photography, that was fine too.

Somewhere along the chilled asphalt south of Prince George we stopped one morning, early, just before sunrise, for a pit stop along the isolated trail leading around lakes, mountains and small mountain hamlets just coming to life for another day where the landscape is big in every way you can describe.

It was cold getting out of the coupe, stiff kneed, seeking relief from coffee along the side of an empty highway. Standing there, relieved, a beautiful panorama unfolded over the roof of the Mustang. Referred to in photography books as "Motif #3" this cobalt blue lake and mountain scene captivated me for the longest time and I stood there just taking it all in.

I knew what I had to do. I had no tripod, or the desire to even set one up, so I used the car roof. Only one frame on the Nikon was exposed and it's a miracle I got that one off. I had never seen anything as awe inspiring as this in any of my travels.

STH

The rest of the trip was great, with another week on the road before Will and I split up and I headed home. I hadn't given the scene any more thought. It was good to get home to my family. Then the chromes came in and a part of me was taken back to that morning along the shoulder of an empty highway at dawn.

Many, many cibachromes were made and given to friends. I've never offered *Blue Lake* for sale. Tonight, sitting here looking at the blues of reflected mountain and

Fellow traveller, Will Pardew, admiring Blue Lake, in 2012. Photo by Todd Holden.

lake, the effect is as strong as the day I first saw it.

Sitting here now, recalling that day, I wonder if I really took the photograph. I wonder if Will took it with my camera. What if he snuck into the gear bag and took the photograph and never told me. What if....? Nah.

========== 30 ==========

Todd Holden writes from his home, Rustica, and took one other trip to Prince Rupert, by another route through Lethbridge, Calgary, Banff and Jasper where he and Will were under Mounted Police guard over night.

Big Hearted Pups and the Love

For some, the love of a spouse or the closeness with your children is all you crave. It truly is a gift to be cherished...for many, the unconditional love between a dog and his master is something that remains a refreshing alternative to the closeness of family.

In the morning as the sun creeps over the evergreens and into the bedroom windows, one of the three of us wakes up and lets the others know the day has begun. Sometimes it's Frisco, the matriarch of Rustica... at nearly 13 she often rises first, both thirsty and wanting to go out (hopefully) for her morning constitutional.

Frisco and Dude keep an eye on the place and I keep them company. Photo by Todd Holden.

Some mornings it's the Dude who stirs first, as he's cuddled in my folded right arm and the pillow. He is a pleasant 'morning' pup, as is Frisco, both easily relaxed and just wondering what the lug in the bed is going to do first.

This morning as I took in the love of these two pals, words started running through my head, and I reached for the notepad on the nightstand. I wrote down my thoughts so that I wouldn't lose them once I got up and started moving toward the day.

"Animals have been our greatest guides...braver than knights...protective and possessive...devilish like children, ornery with a mess now and then...yet so very wise and tuned in to our human foibles....I learn from them."

Maybe what I meant to say, upon re-reading this, was not 'I learn from them,' but 'we learn from each other.' Surely, they have a way of teaching that is far more subtle but just as effective than any human I know of.

To wit: I have learned to control my anger through these two pups...as mentioned before in these columns, times when I've been seriously hurt and let out a yell, they have reacted in some very telling ways. Once the injury is tended to with peroxide and some bandages, they watch with concern and cock their heads from one side to the other, inquiring silently, 'are you okay?'

If I am angry and go into a rant, they disappear and without further notice are as 'invisible' as pets can often become. After a short time, I calm down and reassess the situation. It is then that I realize Frisco and the Dude have vanished. I call them with a more tender tone of

voice and they make their way back into the room. At that precise moment I look at the both of them and can't help but feel the love they have for me...and I, them.

"They show us that time is so often wasted on fears that could be courageously faced."

So it is with those of us who have had pups, or have them now. Not sure how they earned the term 'man's best friend' but it is true, if only we take the time. As my friend in York, Pa., John 'Roo' Adams wrote when my son's 18year old pup, Koda died, "anyone who has ever had the pleasure and honor to be chosen as a sidekick to our wise and noble four legged sages, can feel your loss."

That's the facts of being with a dog...not owning a dog, or keeping a dog...but sharing a life with a dog where the love and companionship is mutual.

The love shared between man and dog becomes stronger as each day passes.

My editor, Wolf Wallis, has had more than a few dogs in his day and shares the sentiments completely.

"I've had a lot of dogs and I've loved them all. Of the most recent, I had a German Shepherd Husky who had been both physically and mentally abused as a pup. Got him from the shelter when he was about 3 years old. Brought him home and it took more than a month before we heard him bark. I spent the next 6-7 years loving that dog to pieces, bringing him out of his shell

as best I could and just plain treating him right...for all the bad times he had gone through. Maxwell was a good friend and very polite in the household. He died in my arms at the vets after a few months' bout with cancer, but even then he looked at me as if to say, 'I'm sorry for the trouble.'

A few years later, as I sat in my living room recuperating from two significant heart attacks, I looked around at my family and thought, 'Sorry for the trouble.' Maxwell's ashes sit on the shelf; he doesn't bark much, although to this day he still 'says' a lot."

What I have with Frisco and the Dude is a friendship that goes beyond what I can express on these pages. They are there for me when I just want to sit and talk. They are happy too when I pick up the ball to play throw and retrieve. Most of all, we are happy to have each other. What I have with Frisco and the Dude is between us. Then again, many of my close friends have warm friendships with their dogs and that certainly warms my heart.

Matter of fact, the whole 'man and dog' thing is about 'heart'...and love and respect. Mark Twain had a comment that seems the way to end this scribble. "If you pick up a starving dog and make him prosperous, he will not bite you. This is the principal difference between a dog and a man."

========= 30 =========

He Was Still Dipping at 88...
The Arctic Circle's Ellis Reeves

Ellis Reeves. Photo by Todd
Holden.

Time was when folks drove east on Route 22 past Churchville there was enough food, cars, golf and good times to last a lifetime. Those days are not the same since the Big M Drive In and Outdoor movies have folded up and the Aberdeen Cattle Auction is no more.

One standout, however, continues to grow in popularity and it all began in 1966 when Ellis Reeves stopped selling ice cream in Washington and took over a 'soft ice cream' stand in Churchville.

"I had tough times, no work, so I went to work for Freezey Palace driving an ice-cream truck in the Nation's Capitol. I hated that job...a rat race...so after two years of it I quit and came to Churchville to run the Arctic Circle."

Today, at 88, Ellis can still dip a double cone or whip up a snapping good double thick milk shake, but he prefers to pass time playing a few hands of gin rummy

with his pals. Pals dwindle when you hit his age and
Ellis has decided to turn over the operation of his 'baby'
to one of his sons, Richard.

So just how does one get into this business? "For
starters, I worked with my brother in law, Fred Bennett,
in a Twin Kiss soft ice cream place on Martin Boulevard,
in Essex. Before that I farmed here and there," he notes.

Sometimes, destinies turn on a dime and when the
Big Cone came up for sale, Ellis Reeves began spinning
the wheels. "There was a little ice cream stand on Route
40 in Havre de Grace that came up for sale and I bought
it in 1956. My lawyer, Brodnax Cameron, Sr., in Bel Air,
set up the financing for me and said he'd back me.

"You better make a go of it, because I don't want to be
down here selling 'shaving cream'!" Cameron told Ellis,
referring to the soft type ice cream, which was relatively
new at the time in these parts.

Soft Ice Cream was the trademark of the Big Cone,
and so it became the trademark of the Arctic Circle as
well. Ellis and his wife Madge bought their second 'soft
ice cream' establishment in 1966.

The timing was perfect for the clientele of movie
goers, fast cars and pretty girls...everybody screamed for
'ice cream' and Ellis' was the place to go for it.

The combo of the Churchville Drive In and the Arctic Circle proved to be a winning combination for years. Folks would let out from the movies and head straight across the street to get an after-movie treat. Then again, chances are, if the drive in hadn't been there, Ellis Reeves' ice cream stand would still have kept a long line of customers at its order windows. Long before the malls and the super stores came to town, families would pack up the kids for a pleasant drive to get a treat at the Arctic Circle.

Perhaps even more significant is that before they were families, plenty of young folks would meet at the Arctic Circle to get a milkshake or ice cream and catch up on the latest, check out the wheels and otherwise socialize in ways that are mostly unheard of these days.

Adjacent to the Arctic Circle is the Churchville Golf Driving Range and miniature golf. It proved to be a welcome neighbor for Ellis and Madge. Today, batting cages have been added to the golf center. Across the street, in the old cattle auction barn, archers practice their skill with bow and arrow.

The burgeoning Arctic Circle called for more time on Ellis's part, so he leased the Big Cone to his step son, Gary Williams, and the soft ice cream parade was on.

At the same time Ellis had three Freezey Palace soft ice cream trucks on the road....the first in Harford County.

STH

"I really had a tough time with that, so after two years of the trucks on the road, I came back to the Arctic Circle and I've been here ever since. Another son, Van, ran the Big Cone until his 'regular job' took him to Germany. So that's when I closed it down," Ellis said.

That location is now occupied by Rita's Desserts. Another son, David, ran the Arctic Circle with his dad and Richard until recently.   Now it's just Richard with Ellis coming in from time to time to make sure things are 'just right'...and judging by the crowds, things are 'right as rain' and Ellis is satisfied that he's done a good job, with a good product and even better service.

It's a small location, but a pivotal location. The only phone is a pay phone in the lobby, and to order carry out, you have to call that number.   A few benches outside offer the traveler a spot to sit and enjoy a number of carry out items, including great hamburgers and every day a blend of Ellis' special homemade soups.

"I was held up once, was working by myself one winter's night. A masked man with a gun on me emptied the register and took my wallet...told me to lay down on the floor...I knew then and there I was a dead man...I thought 'This is it!' and then the crook was gone.

"Never caught him...and it took me years to get over it...He actually jumped over the counter and held the gun on me. Terrible thing to be robbed."

The good times far outweighed the tough ones, and today the families that go to play miniature golf and have a treat are offered a glimpse of the 'good old days' in Harford County.

"I like to come in, help out where I can, and do book work," Ellis says. "I played a lot of gin rummy in the back room with Bill Garrett, Bill Weaver, Charlie Walter, Bill Osborne and Pete Moxley, but I never played you," he said to me as we concluded the interview.

Ellis Reeves stands with his son, Richard Reeves, in front of Ellis' prized Camaro. Photo by Todd Holden.

I will play a hand or two with Ellis for sure. As I left he asked if I wanted a milkshake..."made by the master and it's the best shake in the county," he laughed. To tell the truth, it was and he is.

========= 30 =========

Wondering Where
The Songbirds Are

I was thinking the other day; folks still stop and mention the birds around their homes and businesses to me. They still ask me questions that sometimes are just common sense or other times even a puzzle for me to figure out. What I will tell you is that no matter how simple or off the wall, every question is just as refreshing to hear as the bird questions I received 35 or more years ago. I suppose when the questions stop coming I ought to worry. Till then, thanks for asking and it's my pleasure.

Every now and then it's fun to share these observations with you, the readers. After all, that's what the folks in my life share with me, so why not share with you.

Hello Todd,
I am curious if you are experiencing the same phenomena at Rustica.

There are hardly any birds coming to my feeders. The suet blocks in past years had woodpeckers fighting over them...only an occasional bird now.

The thistle seed socks...nothing. All summer long had more goldfinches than I could count. Previous winters had loads of house finches, golden-crowned kinglets.

Wondering, what's up, no birds...nada. Not even seeing any dark eyed Juncos.

The regular seed feeders have nothing. No cardinals... now that is hard to believe.

My neighbor told me the same thing in her feeders. What is going on?
Gary

Birds aplenty here Gary...woodpeckers hammering suet...chickadees, nuthatches, titmice, juncos on the sunflower.

Haven't been filling the feeder as much though...but with the warm weather and the rains, some 'natural food' is still around...after the past night, colder, things should pick up. I think it has to be weather related...the birds are here...especially the hawks.

As I reply to your quandary, chickadees are on the feeder now...big time. Downy, hairy, red bellied on suet, during the mid morning...and a sapsucker the other day, just one day, but he was there...neat bird.

Gary, keep in touch on this.
Bird

The following day, this note from Bob Chance, near Darlington.

> *Bird, got out and enjoyed the warm weather. Stopped on Basin Run Road and fished for a minute. A dozen cardinals and a Rufus-sided towhee defended the bush line. Kermit (Updegrove) taught me well.*
> *Bob*

Well, Bob, he most surely taught us both well...I owe much to him and Wilson Ford...many lessons learned by masters in their own right.

So many birds identified by song not sight or color... when all three are in the mix it's a gift from Heaven...to us earthly mortals. Absent of that, it pays to remember what we were taught. Listen first, and listen closely. They'll come to you if you're patient.

Point is, regardless of the activity at your feeder now, just keep it filled and make sure the ports are clean and open. Those clogged ports can send the feathers flying. Weather like we've been having brings in an unusual species now and then, a 'visitor' that may be here a day or two and then gone.

The bird talk is just a part of it. Life in the great outdoors is just not something you can learn overnight. I've been blessed to have had some of the older ones teach me so that I may pass it on. As I've gotten older myself, I haven't forgotten how important it is to listen.

Doesn't matter if it's a bird or someone you've known
for a long, long time. You never know who will write
the next 'good thing'...folks amaze me when they write
expressions from the heart. The late Billy Gilbert was
well known and well liked by many in the area. I hadn't
thought about Billy for some time, as time seems to take
away a recollection or two. He was a wonderful man
who lived and worked the earth. But I recently heard
from a fella who worked here and helped build my home.

> *Mr. Gilbert was a great guy to work for. Never a bad*
> *word. I will never forget Mr. Gilbert as long as I live.*
> *I loved to play with all the dogs they had over the last*
> *almost 30 years. Smooth waters on your last ride home*
> *to our father's house. We will all see you there when*
> *our boat comes for us.*
> *Joe Walls*
> *Street, Maryland*
> *December 28, 2011*

You just never know, and in Joe's words we find
sincerity and love for someone who meant a lot to lots of
people.

As I close off this note, John Magness is out in
the cornfield, picking this year's crop. It is dark, he's
working with his son, Parker, and they always do a
great job of caring for this sacred land that brought such
bounty to our farm back in the day.

STH

The songbirds will come back Gary and the earth will keep on turning. Sometimes you just have to listen a little closer to the song.

Photographer unknown.

========= 30 =========

Basic Rules for the Clothesline, Part II

A while back I wrote a column, The Clothesline Saga, wherein the fundamentals of hanging clothes on the line to dry in the breeze and sun were discussed. Some time later I was given by a reader of the Star, the 'basic rules for clotheslines'...some of which I can accept, some of which I can't. To each his own, but when it comes to hanging clothes on the line there isn't much wiggle room to hang on.

You may agree, or disagree, depending on if you even enjoy the pleasures of the clothesline saga. The reader's observations appear below, with my two cents immediately following.

THE BASIC RULES FOR CLOTHESLINES
1. *You must hang the socks by the toes...NOT the top.*

Right off the bat I disagree with this one. I clip the top edge of the sock, not the toe. Why? They dry quicker this way.

2. *You hang pants by the BOTTOM cuffs...NOT the waistbands.*

Again, I disagree. I hang pants by the belt loops, inside out, and they dry better.

*3.   WASH the clothesline(s) before hanging any
clothes - walk the entire length of each line with a damp
cloth around the lines.*

Totally correct...my mom taught me to do this,
and she had a stainless steel clothesline, you can
really see the dirt that accumulates on the line
when you wipe it clean.

*4.   You need to hang the clothes in a certain order, and
always hang "whites" with "whites," and hang them
first.*

Partially true...I 'group' items, for ease of folding
when I bring them in. But I've never been so anal
to follow a certain order. A little here and there is
acceptable.

*5.   NEVER hang a shirt by the shoulders - always by
the tail! What would the neighbors think?*

Agree 100%, but I don't care what the neighbors
think. Then again, that rule was 'then and this is
now.'

*6.   Wash day on a Monday! NEVER hang clothes on
the weekend, or on Sunday, for Heaven's sake!*

Partly correct, however weather plays a big part
in when to do laundry and hang it outside. Even
in the winter months, if we have a warm day, I do
laundry so I can hang it on the clothesline.

7.   Hang the sheets and towels on the OUTSIDE lines
so you can hide your "unmentionables" in the middle
(perverts & busybodies, y'know!)

Usually I do towels, washcloths, bed linens in
one big washing. I'm not really sure I have any
'unmentionables'...at least not any more since the
ladies have moved out. Actually, when ladies
did live here, it was kind of a trophy to have their
'undies' on the line...if you know what I mean.

8.   It doesn't matter if it's sub-zero weather... okay to
hang clothes when it's cold because they "freeze-dry."

Partly true, but once inside they were still 'wet'
and that was against my rules...nothing damp
folded...fear of mildew. EEEWWWW!

9.   ALWAYS gather the clothes pins when taking down
dry clothes! Pins left on the lines are "tacky"!

True, but then again I never professed to be 'un-
tacky'...my pins stay on the line, and the wooden
ones last far longer than the multi-colored plastic
ones.

10. To be efficient, you should line the clothes up so that each item does not need two clothes pins, but shares one of the clothes pins with the next washed item.

True, although not preferred. In a pinch I have done it this way, but if you've got the clothespins, use them.

11. Clothes off of the line before dinner time, neatly folded in the clothes basket, and ready to be ironed.

Partly true again...clothes off the line by sundown, 100% of the time, gently 'gathered' and brought in to the sofa, where they are folded. Ironed?...well, that was then and this is now.

IRONED???!! Well, that's a whole OTHER subject! I have an iron here, a 'steam-dry' iron...I think it's been used by some of the ladies who have lived here. Maybe once I used it, but not sure for what. It's a good iron. Also have an ironing board, and used to use it to 'air dry' resin-coated black and white photographs that I had printed.

========= 30 =========

Saga of the White-Albino Stud Bullfrog and the West Texas Groundhog

A nimal stories come and go and from time to time we learn a little about some unusual creature behavior, like just how far an owl can turn their heads around or why a dog howls at the moon. Sometimes our own behavior is often mirrored in that of a turtle, a gull or a groundhog.

Filling the bird feeders this morning and walking the expanse here at Rustica, I observed various winged and footed creatures or at least markings of where they had been. As I steadied my gaze across the field, the saga of the White-Albino Stud Bullfrog came to mind. Strange thoughts will occur when you are out in nature and this was no exception. I first heard of this interesting creature from a man by the name of Stanley "Monk" Chilcoat who was living on Williams street in Bel Air back in the fifties.

Monk had heard of this special bullfrog from pals like Roy Lloyd and Buddy Lyons, at Boy Scout meetings held over at the O'Neill homestead, Dungannon also near Williams street. Harry St. A. O'Neill was our Scoutmaster but I don't think he knew of the albino bullfrog. Not many folks did. It was really more or

less folklore for young boys who camped out, ate baked
beans and uncooked Vienna sausages, and slept in a pup
tent along one of the many streams in the area.

I recall as a youngster hearing wild tales of how
the White-Albino Stud Bullfrog was commonplace in
this area. Some say he was carried across the ocean on
a slave ship, while many believe this was a zoological
cross-breeding experiment gone bad. The way Monk
described it, the White-Albino Stud Bullfrog was a
nocturnal creature that could grow up to a foot in length.
Some say he could easily jump six to ten feet and lived
in the hollowed out crooks of trees. Much of this lore
was passed along during camping trips to Broad Creek
Memorial Scout Camp by the lads tenting on Flint Ridge.

Then there was the West Texas Groundhog,
commonly mistaken for an armadillo; however, this
particular groundhog was known for eating its young.
Naturally, the West Texas Groundhog, a sleek and fleet of
foot also nocturnal creature, became extinct some years
back.

I never actually saw either of these creatures Monk
spoke of and as I've grown older, I'm beginning to
suspect my leg was actually being pulled by Monk as
opposed to a bullfrog or a groundhog. If it's an albino,
it's gotta be white, right? No matter, I do keep a lookout
for these two oddball animals and if they happen on
the property, I'll likely try to catch them or at least snap
a picture. The Dude and Lady Frisco also may happen
across these and other creatures.

All this brings to mind the art of Delta's own, Dave DeRan, of Pikes Peak Road. Like me, Dave is enamored of all sorts of wildlife and produces exceptional artwork to share with the world. This year's final showing of his artwork will be held at his home, as usual, with fine 'munchies' and blue-grass sounds emanating from all over the house. Mark your calendars for December 4th, from 1p.m. till 5p.m. The theme this year is 'Spots, Dots and Pointilles.'

The paintings of spotted turtles are incredible, capturing the overhead view of a turtle crawling, legs extended, neck and head stretched as far as can be... we've all seen this behavior when first we come upon a crawling turtle, and Dave has captured that 'precise moment' in his paintings. Do yourself a favor and drop by on the 4th and see for yourself. It's totally a breath of fresh air and who knows, you might run into someone you haven't seen in a while.

I don't believe Dave has yet observed and immortalized the White-Albino Stud Bullfrog or the famed West Texas Groundhog. Then again, maybe he has and is just keeping them under wraps for a future showing of his work.

Life's a crap-shoot when it comes to surprises, especially in nature. Just ask Dave DeRan or Monk Chilcoat, or even Buster Bigelow.

========= 30 =========

Consecration Of
Falling Pine Needles

Waking and walking out into the fresh sunshine just now peeking through the branches early on this brisk, fall day, there is ceremonious splendor as I and my pups greet the morning. It is magical this time of year, with the crispness and humidity-free fresh air opening the day. The pups run ahead of me and down the steep steps, the ones that Jack Poole cussed the day he carved them out when this house of wood was built in 1984.

Frisco and Dude are well ahead of me to answer nature's call, as I will too, once I join them outside. It's funny watching them angling for position to wrangle out through the mudroom, the small space separating the laundry area from the outside. The three of us jockey for position in the 'air lock' and as I open the door, they run out onto the cold concrete of the garage. From there, they bound outward onto freshly fallen pine needles from the huge white pine that has suffered many amputations over many blizzards and heavy snowfalls.

Each of us hits a favorite spot out by the tractor shed or past the big locust, also planted the same year as construction began here at Rustica. As I finish my morning salutation, Frisco sits nearby anxiously since she's already hungry for breakfast. The Dude, well he has other business at hand, nothing foul intended...the scent of mice, moles, chipmunks and fox are flooding his sensory canals like no human can imagine.

Should he pick up a scent, he's long gone into the cornfields or snorting around the woods. Some mornings, he stays close by and sniffs around the tractor along the mower deck or at the hen house inside the tractor shed where oh so many pea-chicks were fledged in previous years here at Rustica.

The ever-faithful white pine standing outside of the tool shed at Rustica and bringing a bed of fresh pine needles every year. Photo by Wolf Wallis.

This morning, Dude is working his way into the field as I hear the corn shuffling and his dog tags jangling that reveal his progress and approximate speed of attack.

I walk a few steps closer to the cornfield so that I can listen for Dude and I am met by the magical pine needles...fallen, falling and ready to fall all around where I stand. I can now welcome this change of seasons as the ceremony is delightfully uncovered before my eyes.

I smell the freshness of nature's beauty as I also recall the feel of this sacred carpet beneath my feet. Nothing, nothing I can think of, is as purely refreshing as walking barefoot on pine needles in the fall. I kick off my shoes, close my eyes and stand in reverence of the blanket of pine needles...for just a moment. The brilliant yellows and tans bring to mind a fresh set of bed linens for the comfort zone of the fire pit. They cover the wooden chairs and aromatic cedar stumps folks use to comfort themselves or sit a frosty adult beverage on when they stop by for a visit. With the pups nearby and a fresh bed of pine needles to stand on, I am smiling upon the morning.

It's a new month coming fast on us, so I go to the calendar inside the tool shed attached to the garage and take it down to turn yet another page and I am reminded of how fleeting this life can be, calendars have a way of doing just that. What to my wondering eyes should appear from behind where the calendar has been left for at least 30 days surprises me. A covey, a cluster, a mob, a

herd, a mess of stink bugs, about 40 or more are bunched
up as a mosaic might be inside an art gallery. They are
all grouped together, silent, motionless and disgusting.
It's an early morning discovery that beats anything
Dude might be finding in his search, still going on at the
perimeter of the cornfield.

The recycling barrel is just under the 'clot of bugs'
so a handy can is easily nabbed and used to brush the
stinkbugs into. A feeling of accomplishment this early in
the day does wonders for the soul, at least for mine. I get
them all except one, and he darts off and onto the floor
its fate sealed by a stomp from my sneakers. I've heard
you aren't supposed to crush them for fear of releasing
some noxious aroma, but I had to act in self defense.
Luckily, I smell nothing but the pine needles.

As for the ones I captured, the can is shaking like a
set of castanets in Desi Arnez' band seen and heard on
'I Love Lucy'...as a trophy, this is the sound of music to
my ears this morning. I am at once struck with devious
thoughts; do I soak a handy napkin in alcohol and gas
the little buggers? Do I crush them with the napkin, and
bring about a quick demise?

There are other thoughts, pure and evil, and none
seem to be the right thing to do. Actually, now that I've
found the stinkbugs I feel a little sorry for them. Okay,
we don't want them around, for sure, but now, after their
hiding place for hibernation has been outed, what is the

best thing to do that will not upset what started out as a beautiful morning? Not a good thing to jinx the day just as it's getting started.

There is an empty, rinsed out Breakstone cottage cheese container in the recycling barrel as well, so I dump the bugs into it, not losing one, and replace the top, tightly and securely, and put it in the barrel. It will be at least a month till my pal, Gordon Smith, comes by for our trip to Scarboro Landfill...and their fate is sealed one way or the other.

I've seen folks waste gallons of water flushing them down toilets, and that's just plain wrong. It's not that I'm afraid a stinkbug will grow the size of an alligator and escape into the city water system, but it seems a waste of water like letting the faucet run while you brush your teeth. Others collect the buggers and place them in Zip-Lock bags, then crush them and toss the bag in the trash. Sucking them up into a vacuum cleaner just doesn't seem prudent.

Stinkbugs are a new enemy, unlike yellow-jackets that have nearly claimed my life on two occasions. This new 'bug' is evil, yet benign in some ways...I haven't really grown to fear or hate them quite yet. Regardless of my sentiments towards these miniature warships, they are in the cottage cheese container, no longer cloistered behind the months long gone on the wall.

STH

I have spent a lifetime harmonizing with nature in my own way, a way of appreciating everything around me...with the exception, just a little, of the stinkbugs. There is no known predator of these armor-covered bugs, at least I haven't heard of any yet. And maybe, just maybe, some beneficial trait will be defined and I will not fight them as fiercely as today. I'll have to ask my daughter, Mina, if she knows of a solution.

I come out of the tool shed like a gladiator entering the coliseum in Rome, triumphant and proud of finding and winning. Dude is sitting beside the fire-pit while Frisco is resigned to a warm spot in the sun flowing over her coat like radiant lighting in a photography studio.

Me? I need coffee, water, anything to toast the day that has started out so well. Standing there taking in the warm sun on my face a light northwesterly breeze picks up and scatters some more pine needles down on the three of us and thickening the sacred bed of soft needles that comes once a year and lasts a lifetime.

A sip of cool water and the sun continues to rain down on my face and my pups. We are ready for the day.

========= 30 =========

So Long Suet, It's Been Good To Know Ya

Time was when I learned of 'pure beef kidney suet' for wintering songbirds. Along with the black oil-base sunflower seed mixed with a little cracked corn, that's all I ever put out every winter.

It was easy to stock up each year when the sunflower seed was on sale, usually $8 for a 50-pound bag. Local butchers like Peppi's and Benson Meats gave the suet away...prime suet...no blood or meat in it...looked like a big bar of Ivory soap it was that pure.

Grocery stores always had the little red mesh bags that onions used to come in, and they made great containers to put the suet in and hang from a rhododendron close by the window. This made it quite easy to pack suet into the onion bag, walk around to the side of the house, and find a rhododendron branch that would hold the winter delight.

Life was good, for me and the songbirds. It was a thrill to have downy, hairy, red-bellied woodpeckers visiting the suet on their daily rounds. Some days, the mornings were unusually long and peaceful because of that simple bag of feed for the visitors. I would sit at the computer, drinking a morning cup of joe and welcome the day. Then the woodies would come calling and

pecking at the suet through the onion bag. Usually by the time spring rolled around the suet bags were tattered and ripped and nearly empty.

Folks just took the suet for granted I guess...it was a good treat for the 'meat eating birds'...the ones who foraged in the trees for bugs and grubs and creepy crawlers all summer long.

These times they are a changin' as the song goes and good suet is hard to find anymore. Peppi's and Benson Meats are long gone. Super markets no longer have suet, other than little strips that they toss in the garbage.

"We don't get enough with our meats to save any for the birders," Lou, of Food Land, in Churchville told me the other day. "What we get are little strips, not like the old days when we had to cut off big chunks of the stuff."

So it goes, we can buy the 'pre-packaged stuff' but it's not the same as taking an onion sack, stuffing in big chunks of white, pure, beef kidney suet then watching the woodpeckers, flickers, nuthatches and chickadees hammer away filling their gut. The simple suet sack is, I suppose, history and I must search for another way to satisfy my winged friends. Then again, the delight was also mine.

Things change, not always for the better, or for the birds.

========= 30 =========

Tracks In The Snow Tell The Tale

As the falling pine needles showed the way to changing weather, so too the cold winds blow and eventually, we get our first snowfall of the winter season. It may not be a blizzard and oftentimes around these parts a little spit of winter is all you get. Still, whether waking up in the middle of the night or rising at the first light of dawn there is still something magical in seeing the white stuff lay on the branches and cover the lawns and fields. Seasons change, but there's always room to be a child again.

The pups and I get prepared and venture out into the brisk morning air. It's always a treat for me to walk around the home place after a fresh snow and see the tracks of what critters are visiting during the night. This morning, the only tracks I saw close to the house this 'first snow' were those of a lone red fox. Very close, mind you, he padded around by the fire pit right outside the shed, and then stole through the pines and around the drive way to the cornfield, then down to the marsh.

Very good to see what goes on while the pups and I are fast asleep. Dude smelled the tracks and knew there had been a visitor. He started his routine of sniffing out the odor, then hurriedly followed the trail. By the time he got to the cornfield, Dude was off and running, chasing the fox that had long ago departed. Nothing like the chase to get Dude going though and Frisco followed suit. I just took it all in and watched the scramble.

Foxes aren't the only tracks you can spot on the fresh snow. The normally shy raccoon may make a nocturnal visit or there's always the family of deer that lives down by the bottom of the lane off in the woods. But these are the more obvious four-legged critters on the land and spotting fox tracks are perhaps a bit more rare these days. Wasn't always, but Dude and Frisco seemed to have chased them off, I suppose.

I mentioned this to Gary Rinehart, who lives on Goat Hill Road, near Creswell.

"Where I turkey hunt south of Galena on Rt. 213 there used to be too many foxes. Seems the coyotes are killing them off big time.

"There are a lot more coyotes around than you might think. They are very elusive and nocturnal. They kill all foxes met with and eat house cats. Love them."

Gary, as long as I've known him, is a hunter for game that he dresses and freezes for the table. He's never been a fan of a cat that might prey on young rabbits, squirrels, and other game, killing just for the sport of it. Many hunters are in it for the game alone, finding the target and getting the shot off. Then it's on to the trophy.

Sure, there's a time and place for that and I'm not saying anything bad about the sporting side of things. The hunters I've always respected more though are the ones who get their kill to stock the freezer, maybe share some with a neighbor as winter goes on. In the end, it's

survival of the fittest in whatever world you're in and those that are left can leave a few tracks in the fresh snow for others to find.

========= 30 =========

Ever mindful of our devoted readers, we offer some blank spaces for you to scribble, make a grocry list, doctors appointments, doodles, names of old lovers you'd like to call just one more time. Now, you may wonder why we suggest this. Plainly, because we also like to use these blank pages for all manner of memory jogging.

STH

A Birder's Observations

F irst off, setting the record straight, I'm not a bird-expert, nor am I a 'life lister'...actually when it comes to birding, or 'watching birds' as my grandmom used to say, I'm far from anything more than a guest in the environment and keenly interested in whatever comes my way.

For the unfamiliar, a life-lister is a dedicated bird watcher who devotes their entire life to spotting or discovering as many species as possible. Nothing wrong with that. You could do a lot worse than commune with nature traipsing through state parks and woodland carrying the Field Guide to the Birds of North America. But for me, the notion of watching these creatures and studying their habits, providing human assistance where needed...that's where my instincts take me.

There is a hierarchy of birders that I was never accepted into. Maybe it was doing the radio programs for nearly twenty years on both AM and FM stations in the county where I took 'live call-in questions and observations' from a growing legion of listeners. Maybe the serious birders resented this...I really don't know.

What I knew at the time was lots of folks got turned on to watching and feeding birds from their homes and workplaces. It was fun for me as the idea took hold and without the help of Wilson Ford, Kermit Updegrove or Chandler Robbins I may never have really 'caught on' to the sheer pleasure of seeing a new species and figuring out what class it was. These men, all seminal figures in my life, guided me and I suppose cultivated an interest in me that lives to this day.

So it was, one day while taking a quiet walk in the woods, I spied a Rufous-sided Towhee. The plumage, the way this beautiful bird presented itself...well, then and there I was hooked on birding. What had begun as a curiosity, then a keen interest, became a fascination that lives to this day. The picture below is pretty much what caught my eye so many years ago.

One look at this Rufous-sided Towhee and I was hooked for life. The call of this bird sounds like it's singing, 'Drink your tea.' Photo by David Dube.

It all started with books given to me as a kid. One from the late Sen. Howard S. O'Neill that he inscribed and signed to me for Christmas one year. A book that stunned the eyes of an 11-year-old.

The other book came along much later, maybe twenty years later, when Joan Tapley visited me while I was recuperating from back surgery. It was winter, and she brought me a book of bird photographs to occupy my time sitting in the den of our home in Leeswood. I will forever be grateful to Joan for giving me such a precious gift at such an opportune time.

Hours were spent looking out the window in amazement at the bustle of activity from the winged creatures. In short order, the entire family started paying attention to the songbirds feeding on sunflower and suet.

Living on a dairy farm, our home was surrounded by all sizes and types of birds, from sparrows to hawks, from owls to ducks. The food chain was perfect year round, and the birds were often taken for granted, especially the purple martins, barn swallows and kestrels. My son called kestrels 'the little falcon on the telephone wires' because that's where they would perch in search of food below.

We all have seen what I saw as a kid and later on, it didn't require much, just observations. It was a plus when I could identify a species like the easy ones, cardinals, blue-jays, crows, red-tail hawk...then in the spring it got real tricky with warblers, sparrows and the occasional shore birds that came to the pond.

Throughout the radio days, I kept a journal of trips I had taken to get a 'life bird'...always with knowledgeable folks who verified the sighting. My eyesight was so poor it was really tough, even with a good pair of binocs.

Really, in the end, it didn't matter to me, I let go of the 'life list quest'...I took an attitude that it's the sightings that matter, and the spectacular flight and colors of the birds that really mattered to me.

Materials in the nest include cellophane, feathers, pine needles and spruce twigs, and dry grass...circular contouring nest. Landscaping icon, 'Easy Ed' Hogarth suggested this topic and image. Photo by Todd Holden.

Wilson Ford asked me to help with building and installing bluebird nesting boxes and said to buy a copy of Larry Zelaney's book about bluebirds and how man needed to help with increasing their nesting habitats.

So it was a growing thing, with birds, nesting boxes, and then a Federal permit to rehabilitate injured hawks and owls, and their relatives. One thing overlapped the other. I built a 'hacking house' here on Rustica where the injured often recovered and lived and when ready, left the 'house' to return to their natural environs.

Now, creaking around on a bum left knee, it's hard to walk on uneven ground, so most of my bluebird boxes are close to the lane or pond. I check them regularly because the curiosity is still as fresh as it was 60 plus years ago.

Today, the box on the lane has fledged a brood of Carolina chickadees, so I cleaned out the box and it's ready for another family to start. Cavity nesting birds are the ones who 'take to the boxes' and that's because without the nesting boxes, they would nest in crooks of a split-rail fence post, or a hole where a tree limb has broken off.

Funny, but as I walked outside with Frisco and Dude this morning, over by a tall oak in the yard I could hear the distinct singing of a male bluebird. Singing his butt off...happy, a mellow song...and there is no bluebird box in that area. There's a black locust, some Norway Spruce, a Paulonia, and the big oak.

STH

An Eastern Bluebird is a beautiful winged creature and this one sits atop one of the bluebird boxes along the lane. Photo by Todd Holden.

At that moment, I didn't care where the nest was, it didn't matter. The bird was there, singing and that meant the world to me.

Often we don't need to 'know,' just to 'see and hear'... things have a way of going full circle. The joys of hearing the bluebird's song kept me in tune with nature for yet another day.

========= 30 =========

Massacre At Scott Creek

What started out as a trip down memory lane turned out to be a rude awakening to the present and sadness of Scott Creek, meandering along the Ma and Pa railroad line and Bunker Hill Road, just north of Delta. There isn't a whole lot of childhood left except in the mind, so I grabbed a chance to reconnect with this piece of history. It is still part of the landscape and I would think something the townsfolk would want to preserve.

As a kid I would walk the rails from the slaughter house, out and around the bend of the tracks to the ever-so-long wooden trestle as the line headed north to its final destination of York. In the distance was the long trestle I would try to walk across after a train crossed. It still looks as long as it did when I was a kid. Moss has aged the wood...the rails long since taken up... a few large trees have fallen across parts of it, and still it stands, beautiful and strong and bold as ever. I remember slow moving freights at the station, loading or unloading, and I would race down Bunker Hill Road so I could get a good look as they crossed over the trestle.

Once I saw a couple men, down under it, but I kept moving and headed home as soon as the train passed over. The trestle is maybe 20 or 25 feet at its highest point. Looking at it today was like a page from an old book...read long ago and partly forgotten. It was coming back with each bend of the road and it was good.

The trestles on the Ma and Pa Railroad as it travels along Scott Creek. Dilapidated and neglected, it still brought memories of childhood. Photo by Todd Holden.

Rumor had it that a 'hobo jungle' camp was located beneath the trestle where the hoboes living there could take advantage of the water of Scott Creek and the handouts of folks who fed them for a day's work. A couple of times Grandma Holden took the offer of help from these 'land dwellers' with work around the house and gave them a meal. Sometimes she just packed up some food and gave it to them.

As a 9-year-old, I'd watch the stranger with well-worn clothes disappear down the alley and onto the tracks, walking gracefully across the ties and then out of sight. It was like the circus was in town for a few minutes.

These 'mystery men' appearing at the door on a warm summer's day offered to do odd jobs for some food, and soon after they were on their way.

I never saw the same man twice, but I wasn't living at grandma's full time either. My visits got me there by way of the Ma and Pa train on Friday afternoon, and the same train took me home to Bel Air on Sunday afternoon. I feel grandma took in just about anyone who needed a hand and had an empty stomach.

The two big attractions for me in Delta, apart from Glackin's Esso station, were the Green Marble quarry at one end of town, and the trestle and slaughter house at the other.

I hadn't been near Scott Creek or the trestle in many years and so I turned off of Watson Road and onto Bunker Hill and headed into town the back way. Sadly, the first thing I saw was a couple sofas that had been dumped along the creek side of the dirt and slate road. But the beauty of seeing the creek and old railroad bed took me back into time and a space of being a child exploring the far reaches of the world of Delta in the early fifties.

There's something magical about abandoned rail lines, those flat open spaces of the roadbed, winding along gracefully following the creek in gentle, abstract curves.

STH

The early morning rain had left the dogwood, beech, oak and sycamore glistening with a bright shiny glow. There was no trash strewn about when I walked here as a kid, just water, trees, and trains. The scattered patchwork quilt of blue, white and green plastic jars, gallon containers and shopping bags stood out so terribly wrong in this otherwise tranquil scene of bygone days.

Came to mind that Delta has a recycling center, at the site of the Green Marble Quarry, yet there were bags of trash increasing as I drove along towards town. Why take the time to bag it up, and instead of taking it to a place where some, maybe most of it could be recycled, instead it's tossed like a sheaf out and over the banks of a lovely creek to be scattered across the fern and lichens of the forest floor. Why?

The landscape now unfolds over the next little hill with more bags and sofas and recliners, tables, refrigerators, stereo cabinets...a veritable 'rummage sale' of unwanted household furnishings. These items once served a purpose and when worn out or replaced were destined for Scott Creek, a handy place to toss away what was not wanted.

The 'low spot' literally and figuratively came half way to town, where a large mud hole filled with water caused a little 'jerk' in the road. There were dozens of sofas and furniture, piled up, rotting, soaking wet and stinking. Every color you can imagine on the downhill side of this graceful lane.

The trash kept coming stronger and stronger as it laced the slopes of green. It reminded me for a moment of Christ being crucified on the cross...the trestle, the beams, the innocence of it all and the carnage of raping the land with unwanted things. Like defecating on the face of nature. A curse on those who lay waste to the sacred grounds of Scott Creek and the Ma and Pa trestle.

Before I knew it an hour and a half had passed on this jaunt on Bunker Hill, a short ride but a long process of thought and nerves and sadness. Another bit of looking at the long curve in the roadbed leading to the trestle and I headed out, seeing the town ahead.

Instead of driving up to Main Street for some great ice cream, I followed the well-mowed roadbed along its route south, passing beautiful backyards all well-manicured and cared for. Old basketball nets, tin roofed sheds, ramshackle garages, leading up to a solitary vacant two-story house with a slate roof and a long-gone porch. I remembered this house, where John Wales had his woodworking shop in the back, attached. It was Number 204 Park Avenue and just up the street was the house my grandmother Holden once lived in.

A journey of fifty years occurs in the span of a quiet Sunday ride on the back way to town. A ride a long time in the memory and a long time keeping close to my heart. The sadness of the trashing and massacre of Scott Creek is not right. A group could muster some dump trucks and a backhoe with a cable to haul the debris up and out and it would be a start on keeping a safe walking trail along the history of Delta alive and well.

For now, if you read this and have dumped along Scott Creek, do me a favor and next time you replace the sofa or table, head down to Scarborough Landfill and let them do the dirty work...don't put the dirty work on a treasure. Better yet, take a walk down to Scott Creek and take a good look...it's your back yard.

No doubt there is more to learn about Scott Creek and Bunker Hill Road, and as I am informed, so too will the message be passed along to you, the readers, who need to be informed.

Of course, nothing may be done, and still the beauty of what is there will continue to be overshadowed by man's dishonor to nature and beauty and all things creative.

========= 30 =========

Just A Sip Of 'Fox Grape Wine'

J ust like Christmas, Thanksgiving, Easter and
Mother's Day, once a year in November, I have
trekked to Slate Ridge Post #182 in Whiteford for the best
oyster roast in the world.

Bold statement you might utter...well, utter on if
you will...for pure soul, great company, fantastic cooks
and roasters, shuckers and slicers, Slate Ridge has been
the bench mark for this punk for over 43 years. Earlier
columns no doubt mentioned Bill Rinehart, Grier Pierce,
Gary Rinehart and a couple others I can't recall, taking
me to my first roast, my first ever raw oyster sliding
down my throat, electrifying and scary, then pure taste
sensation.

Yes...only those years when the roasts had to be
cancelled did I miss those events in Whiteford. Now to
be correct, Post #182 also has an oyster roast in March,
and it's a fine one too. Years past, when I did the oyster
roast they had it in the little house out back, with an
overhang where the fire-pit was, where many oysters
were prepared. We often stood while it was snowing,
and enjoyed a beer and raw and steamed oysters.

Today, the Post Home is updated, with a warm room,
but still with an outdoor pavilion with wooden picnic
tables to share with others you might know, and some
you meet for the first time. Some of the old guys are

STH

gone, passed on, as it goes when we get on with age. My son and a couple of his pals enjoy going with me these days, that suits me just fine.

He drives...we hit the steamed, raw, stew and veggies, then cruise Delta, the old haunts he's heard me mention over the past 43 years, then it's back for a second round of steamed and perhaps a sip or two of fox-grape wine, with a little 'white kicker'...smooth!!

This year, there were a couple extra cups of the fox-grape medicine...yes...that capped a great day.

I can't mention all the old pals who still are there, like clockwork, every year...Ross Blake, Caneman Whiteford, Robbie Martin, Jimmy Dawson, Rich Tarbert, Rick Coleman and Lance Whiteford.

I would be remiss if I failed to mention Jimmy Williams. What a character. He's also a mainstay at the roasts. I still remember the time I met him. He called me at home when I worked for *The Aegis*, I didn't know him, but he knew me. Told me he had just shot a big buck and wanted to know if I wanted to put a photograph of it in the paper. I said, "Sure, come on down." He pulled into our lane in Leeswood and there in the truck was a big, 16-point buck. I had never seen a white-tail that big but I didn't want to do a portrait of it, laying in the back of a pick-up truck, so I asked Jimmy if he could 'shoulder it' and carry it out of the woods behind my house.

I figured in the paper that week it would look like I was right there with Jimmy when he shot the buck. He managed to put the buck over his shoulders and the picture was perfect, made the front page that week, and Jimmy likely still has a copy of it. Jimmy is retired from the department of public works for Harford County.

Greeting Jimmy Williams at this year's Slate Ridge Oyster Roast at Post Home #182. Photo by Sam Holden.

Every year Jimmy spots me coming in and gives the best greeting anyone could ask for. Thank God Jimmy is still with us. And thank God for the Slate Ridge Post #182 Oyster Roast.

========= 30 =========

Travelers From The Limelight

My heart is telling me...I love you still

We played some good golf, we loved our dogs, cared for our moms, lived the solitary life, did our own laundry. What a pair we became...when i took Billy Marshall with me for Thanksgivings he fit right in, like an other-worldly uncle...my kids loved him.

For all the good times we spent in later life, we were different. Billy preferred to stay 'out of the limelight' on our rides home from playing a tough round of golf and celebrating. Bloody Mary mornings before a round of golf, a ritual for the victors, no matter the score. We laughed when we made mistakes, we were winners, and we were 'something!'

One time I was taking him to the doctor and a car nearly hit us, speeding through the parking lot. I gave chase, caught the guy getting out of his car and let him know I wasn't happy. Billy just sat there, and when we left, he looked at me disapprovingly and said, "Now, do you feel better?"

Another night, coming up my lane after playing golf there was a car parked with the lights out, Billy and I looked at each other, and I just backed up and let the 'parker' move on...Billy just smiled his approval because I kept my cool.

STH

I would say I learned from him maybe more than he learned from me.

Who knows, I thought he was single when one day he told me he was still married, but had been living apart for many years. It never entered my mind...didn't need to.

I never heard Billy say a bad thing about anyone. He took care of Wayne Holdaway, and that was a tough chore, but Billy carried on...we scattered Wayne's ashes together the way Wayne wanted it done...a toke, a swig and a few words on the hunting grounds where Wayne spent much time.

Death doesn't get any easier to accept, but it sometimes gets easier to understand, maybe because of the generation we are part of. As we age, we grow old and die, it's just the way it is.

Death is more of a visitor to my contemporaries than say for my children and their children...they are younger and death is less frequent. When we are young, we seem to think we are invincible, that death is something only for older folks.

Still, when someone like Billy passes, the younger mourn as well, because he crosses over generational boundaries. Young or old, Billy touched us all.

When someone we love goes the road Billy traveled we try to understand 'why,' all the while blocking out the

inevitable end to that road. I'm like that, just don't think of the end, just the now.

We tell Billy, "It's okay to let go, to die, you've done your work here, done it well." Those around you know this and are comforted by it, some of us selfishly cry out "Why? Billy, why?" But Billy doesn't hear these cries anymore, he is journeying on, breathing heavily, his strong heart not giving up. We who knew him, loved him, as he loved us.

Billy didn't leave any of us, he was slowly but surely taken away from us on a heart-breaking ride over the past two years. We didn't understand what happened to Billy, we just stuck by him and did what we could, just as he stuck by each of us.

He brought us meals from his kitchen when we were sick and he took care of his mom, Alyce, and Wayne Holdaway without being asked.

He was not 'The Star.' Billy was a devout member of the supporting cast in our lives and in so doing was a larger presence as our experiences with him rolled on.

He shied away from the 'limelight' but was more of a shining star in the universe we live in because of his kindness and unselfishness.

His leaving is not easy to accept or understand. But that's our problem...Billy can't help us anymore. His work is done, and he well deserves eternal rest. We must

STH

let go of a dear pal, a brother, a caring human being who walked quietly among us...so quietly the sound is deafening now that he's gone.

Billy Marshall, on a golf outing in 2008 with the author. Photo by Sam Holden.

So I share with you my friends, the life of Billy...a man who was a good son, a good brother, and a good friend. Who loved and was loved dearly. Who gave all of himself to those he knew. Life didn't always seem to take the path expected, but we worked through hard times and Billy always came through with sincere tenderness. He was pleased we all were his friends to the end.

========= 30 =========

The Other Side Of The Napkin

Lots of times we get the most information from folks we see from time to time at the local filling station or the place where we have coffee or breakfast. These are the men and women who make up the work force of faces we come into contact with only casually, but their impact is often profound and deep when we take the time to recognize it.

Living the solitary life and being retired from the rat race affords the privilege of coming into contact with the 'workaday world' a little more often, seeing folks that we 'know but really don't know' as they go about their business. The folks who 'serve' us when we shop or dine are familiar to us only for the moments we are there.... then we've gone on our way and they remain to help another patron the same as us.

Lots of times we get to know the friendly faces and make conversation with them as most folks want to do when they appreciate those who are there, every day, at all hours, to take care of our needs. We tip them when we leave because we want to, not because we have to.

And so it was recently when a man passed away who frequented the Hickory Waffle House. One of the many servers there wrote me a note recalling some of the characteristics of this man...it was like an informal eulogy and struck me as a fitting tribute to someone who I had engaged in conversation with a couple times, but did not really know much at all about him.

Matter of fact, the first time I spoke to this older fellow, I asked him "How come you are so grumpy?" I didn't have any idea who he was, only that he was sitting next to me at the side counter. He smiled at my comment, because I was asking in a friendly way. I learned his name, and realized he wasn't such a bad guy beneath all that gruffness. He was always by himself and most times left before I did. We really didn't mean that much to each other, and the only thing we had in common was two old guys exchanging 'hello's and small talk.'

Truth is, he had a heart attack and died suddenly. The ladies at the Waffle House were sad the day after, when I came in. They told me Franklin had died. I had no idea his age, but was shocked at this news.

One of the servers wrote me a note shortly thereafter telling me some of the stories the ladies she worked with shared about Franklin.

STH

Memories of Franklin from the Waffle House Servers

The girls of Waffle House affectionately called him 'Franklin.' We never called him Frank, we always called him Franklin and he loved it.

He loved for us girls to write him 'love notes.' He would keep them all in his wallet from all different girls and he would take one out from time to time and show us what another girl wrote, I guess to make us jealous. The love notes were always written on Waffle House napkins and he loved when you told him that you loved him and he would always ask us to write lots of x's and o's at the bottom of the note.

He would take us girls out to dinner. He took me and Ashley out to TGIFridays one night. He ordered ribs and he asked the waitress for a 'dipping bowl.' I had no idea at the time what it was used for but now I understand. Instead of wasting napkins on messy ribs he would get a bowl of water to dip his fingers while eating his ribs.

When Ashley was pregnant with her son Chase, Franklin gave us 50 dollars to put into the baby shower we had for her.

He never just tipped the waitress that waited on him. He would give every girl in there 5 dollars and always tell us that we were beautiful.

Franklin would visit us every day, sometimes twice a day. It seemed that everyone knew him or it might have been that he would talk to a fly on the wall. He had many friends and he loved his life.

The girls of Waffle House would often joke to him that he was like Hugh Hefner. We said this to him because he thought we were all his girlfriends. I told Franklin that he was the Hugh Hefner of Harford County and he replied to me "Yes, but I'm better looking."

So it was, the remembrances of a man I know better now, after another person I hardly knew recalled and eulogized his kindness to pass on a bit of the 'other side of the story.'

We never know where or how we will affect others or whether we really know them or not...what matters most is the path we leave behind. So next time you run into a friendly stranger, pass along a little kindness...you might learn something. Thanks Kendall for sharing. Many of the men who would sit with us at the counter at Waffle House also commented on Franklin. None of them has a computer though. Just a lot of guys who knew him, maybe only from sharing a word or two over eggs and coffee....nonetheless, they enjoyed his company, as did I.

========= 30 =========

Stepping Back, Stepping Up... Learning

Years ago I had some time on my hands in the mornings while working at the studio in Bel Air and a pal, Sam Spicer, had mentioned he was driving a county school bus in his off time. Sounded interesting and I applied. It was just up the road from where I lived.

At the time, there was an intensive training program to drive a school bus and I've heard it's even more so these days. For the class I enrolled in, I was lucky to have the late, great Linda Edwards as my instructor. She was an outstanding teacher who also became a good friend over the years.

Learning to drive a school bus was far different from when I passed my driving tests for a car, a truck and a motorcycle. There were so many things to check out before ever getting in the bus and firing it up at the large county lot in Hickory.

The training and driving was good for me. It made my shooting schedule at the studio a little tighter but the rewards of seeing the children who rode my bus and my 'aide' as we pulled in to the John Archer School lot made it all worthwhile.

Some of the children I picked up on my route through Aberdeen, Stepney, Carsins Run and Level were in wheelchairs and tremendously challenged. I forgot all about my tight schedule and the experience certainly made me more aware of the blessings I had.

Overall, it was one of the best things I could have ever put my time and effort into doing. Today, I miss driving the school bus and the folks who helped me along the way.

So it was just the other day that one of the instructors at the Hickory transportation offices invited me to stop by to listen to a required 'in-service safety meeting.' All drivers have to take these 'trainings' from time to time to keep them up to date and aware. To remain certified, drivers must attend 6 hours of training a year.

I thought of my school bus training years earlier and felt that maybe this would be a good thing to do. I don't think I was ready to sign up for bus driving again, but like everything I get involved with, I thought I might learn something. Today it was Kathie Mayor and her assistants, Joyce Levee and Patti Hankins, presenting a program lasting one hour and dealing with 'focusing on the children' when you operate a school bus.

Indeed, as I entered the classroom the first thing I noticed was the poster on the wall stating, 'The driver's only choice is...what is safest for my students.' I knew I was in the right place.

After a series of 'brush up' demonstrations on how to completely go over all the safety checks before leaving the lot in a school bus, the main program dealt with a

horrific, fatal accident that occurred in Gray Summit, Missouri, on August 5, 2010, and what can happen when drivers are following too close and not paying attention to the road ahead.

Even though I was merely sitting in on this session, it made me more aware of the tragic accidents occurring in our area in just the past few weeks. Horrible, senseless accidents that in almost every instance could have been prevented had the culprit driver paid attention. It brought home the fact that many of these fatal crashes happen because someone crossed the center line and hit oncoming traffic head on.

Leaving a safe distance behind the vehicle in front of you is the safest and most intelligent thing any of us can do. Tailgating is definitely a popular means of aggressive driving these days, and it often results in a tragic accident and loss of life.

Thoughts of Linda reminding me 40 years ago to leave a space behind the car in front...'Count 1 chimpanzee, 2 chimpanzees, 3 chimpanzees...'all the way to five or six...that's the space to leave between vehicles... for safe distances and it's easy to do. Many go by the rule of at least one car length for every 10 miles per hour you are driving, but the message is the same...keep a safe distance.

Problem is with the aggressive folks on the road today. They will pull out and into the gap of safety you've created...all because they are in a big hurry...a

STH

hurry that tosses defensive driving and courtesy out the window. Vehicles are built to go a lot faster and a lot quicker than when I was growing up and folks seem to be wound a lot tighter than ever before. I can sympathize with the pressures of today, but reckless driving won't fix that.

Kathie reminded everyone after the testing was over to 'extend your following distances'...and stay focused. Many of these drivers have driven school buses many years with perfect records. These folks are heroes and demonstrate every day examples of what to do and what can be done to get from one place to another safely.

Here's the deal...I love life, and all my friends and family...and each week we read of tragic accidents and hope it's not someone we know who's in one...I hope that each of you reading this will take away a thought of leaving more room between you and the person in front of you...that you won't tailgate or sink to 'road rage'...just cool it, please...and we'll all be around the family for a long time to come.

Lastly, every person reading this should take a course like the one offered by the county transportation folks. Whether or not you plan on driving a bus, the reminders and images of what aggressive, inattentive driving can result in leave a lasting impression. They did on me.

========= 30 =========

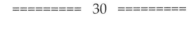

Out Of The Blue...The Spring Luncheon

Getting older has its advantages. You always have a growing list of acquaintances you can call friends. Readers of this column will hear me describe the lives of local heroes gone by or sadly an all too frequent eulogy. I'm blessed to have met so many and their very lives are what make mine worthwhile.

So it was at the Delta Family restaurant on a Sunday a while back that Cellie Hamilton came over to my table and informed me of a great luncheon coming up, where I'd know lots of folks who were there, and yes, the food was really good. She also asked me to be sure to let Danny McLaughlin know too, since he had told her to let him know of the luncheon. She gave me the date and said it was hosted by the Emory Church, a group widely known for their fine meals for various organizations. Like I usually do, I told Cellie I'd check my calendar and if I could make it I would.

Turned out I was clear that Wednesday, so I told Danny to let Cellie know we were on for the 'Emory United Methodist Church Annual Spring Luncheon.'

Often times throughout the county various volunteer fire companies and churches host some really fine feeds, some far better than others. The Emory Church luncheon proved to be one of the very best, at least as far as Danny and I were concerned.

Gathering in the church was like a reunion of sorts, folks from all over the county and across the Mason and Dixon Line trickled in prior to noon. So many faces that I hadn't seen in years greeted me and recalled a story or two. Charlie Head and his wife were there. I hadn't seen Charlie in years. Charlie ran the darkroom at *The Aegis* when I worked there. It was Charlie who kept tossing film up to me on the roof of Boyd & Fulford Drug Store during the 'Great Groundhog Day' fire that nearly wiped out Main Street in Bel Air in 1972.

After comparing the new wrinkles and discussing our respective ailments, Charley and I recalled that eventful day. Charley tossed film up to me, and I tossed the exposed rolls down to him...and the presses were literally 'halted' so the paper would have the best coverage. We were a heckuva team, Charlie and me back in the day.

Another lady came over and introduced herself, saying I didn't know her but I knew her brother. Turns out it was June, the sister of Jimmy Williams. She is Jimmy's older sister and favors him.

Donald and Mildred Blackburn came over. Mildred also worked with me at *The Aegis*. Sort of a reunion within a reunion you might say. And Darcy Lloyd, Harriet Crowl, Joan Heaps, Shirley Harkins, Sally Swahn, Norma and Jim Reeves, among others. So many familiar faces and long time acquaintances. Certainly don't mean to leave anyone out...just didn't take enough notes.

Seeing and recalling was the rule of the day as folks continued to pour into the sacristy. Then Cellie took the microphone and said we would start heading to our tables as she called out the number on our tickets. Very well organized and right on time.

In the dining area tables were set and servers were at the ready. Sitting with us was Herb and Virginia Massey. When they announced the winner of the table decoration it was our table and I gave Virginia the arrangement of colorful tulips.

Served 'family style' the lunch was superb. Potatoes, chicken salad, green beans and an assortment of summer salads. Bob and Joyce Pruitt served our table and couldn't do enough for us.

But it was the green beans that really impressed me. At best, in restaurants, they are either mushy or under-cooked. Usually I have to doctor them with raw onions, but not today.

Found out it was none other than Maryann Hutchins who cooks the beans each year at the church. She has her way of doing the beans, and adds one admonition, "Don't stir the beans!!" Believe me, the folks in the kitchen pay attention for good reason.

STH

Rarely does one run into so many people you know, but don't see that often. That's the charm of events like this one. You go not knowing who you'll see and come away feeling good that you saw so many good people that normally you'd only see at a funeral.

It's true. These are the folks we all remember growing up and seeing around the area. Faces and names that are all blurred with the passing of time. Faces you remember and can't put a name on, which is how it is with me.

Either way the luncheon was superb, for sure Danny and I will be back next year. Thanks to Cellie for filling me in and to all the kind folks who read the column and enjoy it. Thanks to all the servers who made sure we had plenty of iced tea, coffee, dessert and even a spare ball point pen so I could take a few notes.

A lot of the true American spirit lives on in these events held at places like Emory Church...and I'm grateful for it. It was certainly a heartfelt sentiment for everyone there that day just to be among the living...I know that's how I felt.

========= 30 =========

Never Know When A Pup Will Steal Your Heart

My stalwart riding companions, Frisco and Dude. Photo by Todd Holden.

The last thing on my mind, as I took a Sunday ride to Delta to visit my pal Kenkaid, was buying a new Jack Russell pup. I had read the ad by Lucille Rice in the Star...'Jack Russell pups, males & females, shots & wormed, short legs, smooth coat'...and figured a call to see the pups might be good, since I was already in Delta. Like I say, just a ride over to take a look.

By the time I arrived there were only 3 males left. The 'mom and dad' were on the premises, which is always a good sign when looking at puppies. They were

in fine shape, as Dude and Frisco looked on from the truck. They were along for the ride, but just as important they must also approve of any new additions to Rustica.

As I watched the little puppies frisking about I noticed one in particular stayed closer than the rest. I asked Lucille if she'd take a pic of me holding this pup, so I could send it along to my son to see what he thought. This was purely a stall on my part, it takes me forever to buy anything...Scots-Irish, Welsh...who knows.

Lucille obliged and I thanked her, telling her if someone came and took the pup I liked, just call me and let me know...there will be other litters later on...no big deal.

So it was as I started to leave, one fatal glance back in the side mirror at the kennel, and there he was, by himself, standing against the wire, as if to say...'Shucks, I really wanted to meet Dude and Frisco.'

In that moment of clarity my heart ruled my head and overtook me to the point of emotional rescue. The pup had taken my heart in that brief meeting. Surely, it was meant to be.

I backed up the lane and made the deal with Lucille. There was nothing else to do. I asked her if she had a box big enough for the pup to ride in on the way home, and she produced a 'room air conditioner' container suitable for the pup.

So it was that Delta day...sunny and bright and me in the truck with 3 pups...a little trepidation and a lot of joy in the connection made with this pup, the same connection made with Frisco when Barbara Judd had a litter for adoption on Davis Road 15 years ago...the same connection a pup at Daniel Lapp's farm made with me 5 years ago.

The way I do it might be a bit different than most when it comes to a puppy. At Dan's farm when Dude became part of the family, I took Frisco along with me, because after all she was going to have a new roommate so she should be in on the visit. As Dan's kids all came out to be with the puppies on his lawn, Frisco and I got down on the grass with the kids and pups...letting the pups just romp and jump and do puppy things all around.

After a bit, one pup came back again and again to me and Frisco and the bond was made in that instant. That pup was to become Little Dude, as Dan and I settled up.

My granddaughter Scarlett had a field hockey game in Bel Air at 1 pm that same Sunday when I bought the pup from Lucille and it was close at hand. I made the trip back to Rustica, and settled into the yard with the new pup and let him romp with Frisco and Dude....they took right to him.

STH

Granddaughter Scarlett holds Chester, the newest addition to
Rustica. Photo by Todd Holden.

Early on with training we needed a name...preferably two-syllables...and it came to me to name him after my paternal grandfather, Chester Holden....everyone who knew him called him 'Ches'...and it seemed to fit the chestnut browns of this pup.

Chester it was to be...he's a fine pup. At the vets for a checkup and shots, Dr. Claire McNesby, who raised Jack Russell's years ago said his conformation was outstanding and he really was a fine looking pup. So it was another 'good sign'...that a simple ride to Delta, with no intention of actually buying a puppy, came to be.

Why did I do it? One reason is I don't want to be alone here anymore. The pups are companions, they warm my heart with their unconditional love, they ride with me on cruises to visit pals and family...they keep the mice at bay around the tractor shed and home.

They are my best friends...it's all really that simple... the heart rules the head sometimes...and many times it's for the better to just let that happen.

========= 30 =========

Saying Goodbye,
Above And Below Ground

This week, two of my life-long pals were saying goodbye. My bud, Tom Stark, is moving to Albuquerque, New Mexico, in the fall. He's lived here all his life and the time has come, he said, to 'get out of Dodge.' His sister, Noralie, lives there and she's happy with the weather and folks living there.

Tom was the 'wheel man' when we put the skunk in the Bel Air Theater back in 1955. I met Tom and his sister and family in 1953 when my family moved to Southampton Farm near Bel Air. Farm boys had few friends nearby...mostly the boys who worked on the farm with their parents and neighbors like Tom and Roy Choate.

Once we reached the age of 16 and got our licenses, and providing we could weasel the pick-up truck to run errands for our folks, we were no longer 'land-locked' so to speak.

Tom is three years older than me, and that meant transportation for me, and a new pal for him...I was like a younger brother for Tom who had two sisters.

In the innocent hey-day that we shared in Harford County and lower York County, there's not a lot we missed out on when it came to growing up in a farming community.

STH

The other pal, Ron Rill, was more of a golfing buddy, but we always knew each other through Tom Stark....they are the same age and as Tom and I palled around, Ron, a much quieter, reserved lad, sort of added balance to the equation.

Ron and his wife Joyce are leaving their home near Norrisville, and moving to Myrtle Beach...into a brand new home in a brand new development.

You might say I'm not 'losing a friend,' they will just be farther away...but distance means you don't see them at the golf course, or the ball game or in the stores anymore.

When a good pal passes on we don't see them anymore either...we will meet them on the other side one day.

Pals like Lane Hall, Wayne Holdaway, Charlie Brown and a handful of others are gone for good, but that doesn't mean I don't think of them often and recall the days of fun in the sun...glory days when everything was innocent and fresh...days of youthful antics.

So we say good byes, have 'going away parties' for the ones who head south or west...rarely ever north or east.

STH

Comments like, "Oh, you'll come to visit," or "We'd love to have you visit, any time, really!"...seem to never come to pass. Sometimes maybe, but not many times. Folks just move on who once were 'here'.

A former pastor of mine, Reverend Eugene Peterson, who founded Christ Our King Church in Bel Air, once counseled me with these words..."We all have dead friends and living friends...the ones who are gone are still in our minds and our lives as we do things and say things they inspired in us...while our living friends do the same and are still 'here' to be debated and questioned and admired."

It got me to thinking, images of my Dad come to mind and I still talk with him and ask him 'How am I doing, Dad?' Just today two friends told me stories of my Dad. They recalled him in the positive way I hope I'm remembered to my son and daughter when I'm gone.

In both mentions of my Dad today a warm glow of love came over me, like a new chapter in the book that's written from the day of my birth...a book of stories told and experienced by those who know us and know of us in our lives.

Comes to mind the recent exhibit of Dave DeRan's at his home on Pikes Peak Road. Two large works were purchased just above the sofa I was sitting on. As Luci Snodgrass took hers down, suddenly there was a big bare wall just above my head. It didn't bother me a bit. Out of nowhere here comes Dave with a large portrait of his late dad...

"It's kind of moonlit and goes with the theme of the night," he offered as he hung the large framed painting over the sofa.

It's like that when we have this reservoir of images and thoughts in our minds of those folks who are in our lives, forever and ever...above the ground or below.

========= 30 =========

Solomon John Hall, One Of A Kind

Solomon John Hall, plays his Gibson.
Photo by Todd Holden.

Sometimes, a tall tale is nothing but the truth and for Solomon John Hall, there's a lot of truth in that. He owns two houses, one in front of the other, and four tractors at his home in Chiefland Florida, near Gainesville. Living in two houses cuts the cleaning chores in half and there's a perfectly good explanation for the tractors, but we'll get to that. Years ago he had gas enough to get out of Florida, but he said, "I still ain't a goin' cause my car only goes 30 miles an hour, it'll take too long."

He was asked to come to Nashville to play with Billy Grammer and String Bean to a packed house in 1969. Mr. Grammer was a well known country artist who had a little big hit by the name of 'Gotta Travel On.' S.J., as he prefers to be called, has a brother up this way and comes to Harford County every now and then when the mood strikes him. He plays bluegrass, singing and picking his six-string Gibson electric guitar...which by the way he plays with just his left hand.

STH

When S.J. was only 6 years old he was electrocuted and lost his entire right arm. Tragic though it was, he now is 74 years old and can stretch a tale into an hour long epic. He's road worn and weary, talks fast, and can do 'Beer Barrel Polka,' 'Walk Across Texas' and 'SweetJesus'...with the best of them.

His guitar playing is pure and sweet. With nothing short of a gift from above he can pick out a melody that fills out a sound any backing band would be proud to play behind. Not to mention a voice that's pure molasses and could make the top 25 on any country list.

He's seen a lot and done a lot in his time and name drops Opry players like they were second cousins... tucked into his stories of Bill Grammer he'll tell you about encounters with the likes of Skeeter Davis, Bobby Lord, and the Fruit Jar Drinkers. If at first you might think he's pulling your leg, just keep listening to his yarns and you'll figure out the fabric is real.

Then again, he is an admitted 'hog thief'...and may have stolen the truck he hauled them in. As far as those tractors, the reason he has four of them is so he doesn't have to unhook the mower or the bucket loader each time he does a different job...thus a tractor for each specific job.

He interrupts our conversation after nearly every sentence by saying, "You don't believe me, do ya?'" Sure, I believe ya' S.J....just let's get on with your story. With a twinkle in his eye, he continues on and rambles and

spins a story you just aren't sure is the truth or not. Then again, by the time he's done...or at least winds down to take a breath...you're convinced that no man could make this stuff up.

When he eats cake, or likely anything else, he takes out his false teeth to keep them clean and makes no bones about it. Not one to stand on ceremony, at the same time ole S.J. is about the most courteous and respectful fellow you'd ever want to meet.

S.J. is the brother of Ralph Hall, who lives in Port Deposit. Ralph is very proud of his brother, and justly so. He hauls S.J. around when he's up north, to play, sing and tell tales at churches, family gatherings and hoe-downs here and there.

S.J. enjoys a piece of cake...sans teeth.
Photo by Todd Holden.

One of the possible reasons S. J. headed to Nashville and the Opry was perhaps he was on the dodge for hog stealing and needed a break from the home town law. This has to be verified of course, and the only source is, well, you know.

STH

I asked S.J. if he knew the Roger Miller song, "You Can't Rollerskate In A Buffalo Herd?" He said he knows it and can play it.

When he last played in the area, S.J. said between songs... "How's everybody out there doin?" The crowd says good. As he turns to his players and gives them a key to play in, S.J. turns back to the crowd and says, "Well, let's see if we can fix that." He's pure showman, snake oil salesman, working class hero, musician and raconteur...he's truly an original character. If only we had a few more one of a kind gentlemen like S.J., we'd all be telling tall tales...and every one of them true.

========= 30 =========

Ashes and Ice Cream
Billy Bids Farewell

As the song goes, 'You can't always get what you want. You can't always get what you want...but if you try sometime you just might find, you get what you need.'

So it was to be that editor-in-chief, Wolf and I were asked by the late Billy Marshall's sisters, Lyn and Nan, to come to their home on Glenville road at 6 p.m. to spread Billy's ashes on the lower pond and celebrate Berta's 64th birthday. Billy left this world back on January 26 this year and here we were to say goodbye. Throwing a birthday party in for good measure seemed the right thing to do.

Here we were with ten ladies of independent spirit and humor...all in the 'band of sisters' that took care of Billy throughout his illness and eventual death at his home, in his own bed. Lyn and Nan deserve a medal for what they did, not knowing how long or how intense the illness would become. They will forever be angels in our hearts and a ray of Billy seems to come through in each of their eyes. Like windows to the soul.

Speaking of the soul, part of our conversation that day turned to Nan and her amazing abilities as...*The Stinkbug Whisperer.* This is no joke and I've witnessed perhaps what appeared to be Nan communicating with a stinkbug and the stinkbug responding. As Nan came nearer the stinkbug, she softly told the stinkbug 'not to worry, there was plenty of wide, open space outdoors, that not all the world was a place of tissues and vacuum cleaners.' I watched as the stinkbug slowly lifted itself from the lampshade and flew over to the screen door leading to the porch. Nan cautiously walked to the door, swung it open slowly, then off flew the stinkbug, empowered to survive in the big, old world. Nan always has had a way with words.

However, our presence at the Marshall residence that evening was not to ignore the proceedings, but rather partake in a rather timeless adventure of celebrating the passage of time. As Berta marked another year on this earth, we gathered to mark Billy's return to the earth.

A bit of preparation to properly consecrate the matter at hand was all done with a touch of grace. Jeannie had appropriate containers for each of us to carry Billy to the pond and send him off. Ceremonial shooters were also poured and taken with us down to the pond. Saying farewell is never an easy task, but to be shown respect and love is all anyone could ask. Billy had been in a part of each of our lives to some degree or another for many years and now we would pay our respects in the highest order.

As we walked across the greening yard and headed toward the lower pond, I couldn't help but think of Billy riding on the tractor and getting the lawn cut. He was meticulous to a fault and always enjoyed this chore. There was the time he landed the tractor into the pond, but no one got hurt, which was a blessing.

It was chilly and breezy as we made it to the lower pond, tucked away at the bottom of the swale on the property. All was prepared. One of the ladies began to sing a song that, in my recollection now, I just can't come up with the name of it. Everyone was surely caught up in the moment. As the breeze slowed to a standstill, the Lord's Prayer was recited in unison and we each found a moment to open our containers and release Billy's ashes into the pond.

From his shirt pocket, Wolf pulled out a harmonica in the key of C and said, "Here's a little something for Billy." He proceeded to slowly blow on that harp to a familiar tune no one could quite make out at first. As the melody line was played, the tune suddenly became familiar to my ears and I sung along, "You can't always get what you want..." One by one, the ladies joined in, Berta the most spirited, and we closed out with, "but sometimes you just might find, you get what you need."

Each of us felt a bit closer to one another and of course, closer to Billy. At that point, we figured we had given him just what he needed...we headed back to the house and the warmth of the open hearth and good fellowship.

STH

Homemade cake and fruit and ice cream celebrated the passage of time and we consecrated the evening feeling much closer to the soul than when we first started. After a thoroughly enjoyable dessert and lively conversation with the ladies, I looked over at Wolf who had to work the next day and got the 'high sign' to say our goodnights.

On our way home we spotted a beautiful cusp moon on its back, holding the nectar of the Gods, with Venus and Jupiter brilliant and high in the western sky.

"Well Wolf, I do believe we've been adopted by the Sisterhood of the BillyHood...taken in by wonderful gals who all loved Billy, Nan and Lyn...and now us." Wolf glanced over at me and said, "Sure beats the limelight."

Long before Billy got sick he dutifully tended to his mom, Alyce, even building on an addition to his home specifically for her. The love shown to his mother was pure and unconditional. It was in the same bedroom where she passed away that Billy died, surrounded by love and dignity and soulful care. We all should be so fortunate when our time comes.

You couldn't make up a script more poignant than this story of the deepest of human love and devotion to a brother from the 'living, breathing sisterhood' and a couple of brothers too.

========= 30 =========

The Skunk In the Bel Air Theater – Updated, Revised, Factual

The scene of the crime, Bel Air Theater on Main Street in Bel Air. Photo courtesy of the Billy Holcomb Collection.

From the Baltimore Evening Sun, Wednesday, October 31, 1955.

"While not billed as a Halloween prank, a stunt in Bel Air had the smell of one. Two teen-age boys, possibly budding movie critics, snuck a dead skunk into a theater, while several hundred unsuspecting patrons were watching Jeff Chandler in the war picture, 'Away All Boats' at the only Sunday matinee in town."

"The Bel Air Aegis reports that the young men were booked and held for disorderly conduct."

*   *   *

Magistrate Lewis Williams, whose home Corporal Blaine Hans of the Bel Air Police Dept. took the culprits to, also mentioned inciting a riot as a charge. Perhaps that was just to scare the youths. The 18-year-old, the only one with a license and car, and the 15-year-old, passenger, co-conspirator, accomplice, instigator, were about to spend a night in jail.

*   *   *

**From The Aegis,
published on November 1st...**

"Skunk Is Put In Theater"

"Two Bel Air teen-age boys were arrested and charged with disorderly conduct Sunday night after the young men had secreted a skunk into the Bel Air Theater, where several hundred people were watching a movie.

"The animal's presence naturally caused quite a bit of discomfort to patrons, but the culprits were soon apprehended by Town Officer Blaine Hans and were booked to face a hearing before Magistrate Lewis Williams on Saturday."

*   *   *

The skunk had been hit by a car on Fountain Green Road and the pair found it. They gave it a dose of ether to subdue it, rolled it in plastic and placed it under a gray mackinaw belonging to the 18 year old.

The ticket taker that day was Wilson Monks, a linotype operator at *The Aegis*. The manager was Robbie Wallis, sports editor of *The Aegis*. He had just gone home for Sunday dinner with his family when assistant manager, Ed Snodgrass, called asking him to come back, someone "had put a skunk in the place." "I was already in a bad mood and the call made it worse," Wallis said to Snodgrass.

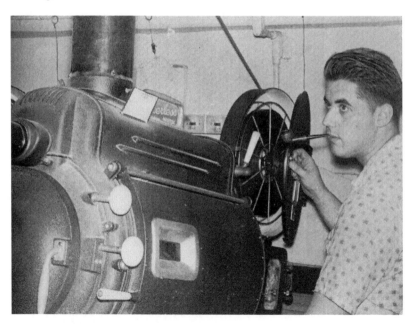

Robbie Wallis in the projection room at the Bel Air Theater. "Find something to charge them with," he told Cpl Hans when the pair were caught. Photo courtesy of the Wallis Collection.

The young man who so valiantly tried to eliminate the odors coming from the front row, center seats was Dickey Terry, son of the infamous Buck Terry, who later managed the theater with an iron hand. In his hey-day, Buck would turn a spotlight in the balcony on anyone rowdy and tell them to leave. This performance on Buck's part, took place while patrons were trying to watch the film.

The pair would never have been apprehended had it not been for the young lady who informed police she noticed a young man with a large stomach entering the theater on the opposite side from the candy stand. Quite unusual for either of the two men in question to avoid the candy counter, that is.

Quotes From The Culprits

Tom Stark recalls, *"I know it was cold, that I had gotten a new pair of hockey skates, and we put the skunk in the freezer bag and then shoved it in the skate box. Actually, I think a car had hit the skunk on Ady road and we were just passing through. We saw the skunk and looked at each other and said, 'The movies.'*

"We went to my house, got the box, and headed for the theater. Every place in Bel Air was closed. The only crowd was at the movies and that's where we took it," this according to the 18-year-old driver, who now resides in Albuquerque, New Mexico, after retiring from his company T.R. Stark Surveyors.

"We went in together, and we'd been around the skunk so long there was an odor, that we weren't aware of, but it must have been covering us like paint.

"Here comes this kid, with a box bigger than himself, smelling bad, hands over his ticket, and he and his buddy head for the front row. We weren't really rocket scientists you know," Stark , a.k.a. the driver, recalls.

From the 15-year-old, who still has great respect for a good practical joke, comes the account of the arrest.

"We sat there instead of leaving. If we would've left then I don't think we'd ever have gotten caught. But we wanted to see what happened. That didn't take too long. Some screams, people getting up and leaving. Some with flashlights timidly looking under seats to see what stunk to high heaven.

"The lady who led police to the culprit, reportedly said, 'Todd, what did you do, bring a skunk in here?'" Stark recalls.

"Todd gets hauled to the back of the theater where he was relentlessly interrogated. Officer Hans repeatedly asked him, "Why did you do it?" To which the young man replied, "Do what?"

In the meantime, the driver was taken by police to the candy counter and grilled. *"I was scared to death, scared that my accomplice was ratting on me. Hell, I was worried I would lose my job at Sutcliffe and Ward. They kept grilling me, over and over, and finally I said, "Look fellas, if it's the skunk you're worried about, we can help you, we know where it is, and we can get it and take it out for you.*

"My plan was for us to go to the skunk, pack it up and escape through the EXIT door at the parking lot. Most of the people had left by then, the theatre was still dark, and the police were right on top of us. The squad car was parked right in front of the theater and they hauled us to Gordon Street, where the Magistrate Williams lived," Stark notes.

*　　*　　*

Commentary

Imagine, these two farm boys, carrying a large box, under a gray mackinaw, into a crowded theater TODAY.....Without a doubt, a SWAT team would descend on the pair as if they were terrorists.

After the arrests, the two were taken to the Sheriff's Office for booking and holding. Then Sheriff Raymond Fulker escorted them to the desk sergeant, Deputy Hood Bowman, who quickly advised the younger suspect, *"You get one phone call, but there's no use calling your dad, he's been notified and told us to leave you in here."*

Mr. Stark, upon hearing this, lost all hope of a career in Harford County. His parents were away for the weekend visiting relatives in Paynesville, Ohio. Years later, Stark recalls, *"My mom, Eleanor Stark, a school nurse and devout Methodist, was so embarrassed by having to appear in court with her wayward son. "It's all because you started running around with that Holden boy," she admonished. "My dad flatly refused to accompany me, guess he was afraid of getting kicked out of the Lions Club,"* Tom laments over the incident.

That night, sitting in a jail cell with his buddy, and desperation mounting, the 15-year-old (one Todd Holden), blurted out, *"Alright then, call Howlett Cobourn or Jimmy O'Neill."* (Havre de Grace and Bel Air attorneys, respectively.)

The two were led back to the holding cell. Both recall it was battleship gray, cold and hard but clean.

*   *   *

Released From Jail

Ultimately, the 15-year-old's father, who was an attorney, came for the boys. According to Stark, the only thing he said to them was, *"Get out in the car boys, I'll take care of this."*

"He had a '54 Ford station wagon, and Todd was in the front seat with his dad. I was in the backseat. All the way to the farm, he kept asking, "Why, why, why...why the hell did you do it?"

"Todd finally summoned the nerve to answer his father, 'Dad, after all the stuff you did when you were a kid, what'd you expect?' His father said that had nothing to do with it, what he wanted to know was why we got caught?"

Stark continued his recollection. "The rest of the way to the farm the three of us planned how to actually get a skunk in the theater and not get caught. I got out at my house; my parents still weren't home from Ohio. I can't remember what happened next. I thought I would go to sleep and it would be all gone by the time I woke up."

Racing through Todd's mind now that he was alone in the car with his father, was whether it would be the glasses that got busted, or the braces on his teeth. No punches were thrown, but as the car pulled into the lane, his father said the first words since letting Stark out, "I'm not really mad at you for what you did son. Just why in hell did you have to get caught?" That was it. He never said another word about it.

My mom was upset because I was taken to jail. She was glad I was o.k. and started to laugh when I told her everything. Dad came in, sat down, listened, and left the room without saying a word.

The first trial was removed because of publicity. Some folks thought it would become a fad, we were admonished, letting wild animals loose in theaters.

The next session was in Judge Stewart Day's chambers in the circuit court.   The two youths offered to pay the manager for refunded tickets and damages.   The manager had calmed down. Judge Day tongue-lashed the pair and told them they were on probation. Then came another lawman, with a special demand.

Police Chief J. Vaughan McMahon, told both boys, now on probation, to turn in anyone in town who had loud mufflers, glass-packs, Dyna-tones, steel-packs, Hollywoods or straight exhausts. To this day, neither of the boys ever was able to think of anyone who had loud mufflers. They had no idea. They were certainly not 'finks' or 'stool pidgeons.'

There you have it. That's just the way it was.

========= 30 =========

Todd Holden lives near Bel Air, and still gets together with his longtime friend, Tom Stark, who owned a survey company in Bel Air and has since left Maryland to retire in New Mexico. They love animals, especially skunks. A few years after the skunk episode; they nearly killed themselves in a car crash on Route 24 driving through the Rocks. Again, Stark was driving. The Triumph TR-3 was demolished after hitting a phone pole and careening off the road into Deer Creek landing upside down in the water.

From retired Officer Blaine Hans...
aka The Arresting Officer

"Todd, I sat here and read this story and tears came rolling out. It's great!! I recall most of what's here, but my memory is getting fuzzy on lots of things anymore. Getting old I guess. I can't think of anything to add. You have it all here. I do recall you both were 'scared to death'...when you were taken into custody.

"One of the things in the story: [calling me] Cpl. Blaine Hans of the BAPD, gives me a promotion I never made. I was never more than an officer with BAPD. Klein (Cpl. Ferd Klein) made the first rank in the department. I was always the peon. Later on, it correctly identifies me as Town Officer.

"I secretly thought it was a great prank. Old Robbie was the one who was keen on pressing charges on you boys. Now, there are some stories I could tell about old Robbie, but not for publication. I wasn't the most proper kid in Bel Air myself when I was a teenager. You boys were no different than the rest of the characters in town. You just had bigger plans, took a bigger chance...and got caught...the cat was out of the bag. Well, the skunk anyway. The story took on a life of its own."

=============

Tom Stark recalls that when the police called Gwynne and Jean Holden reporting their son's arrest they were nonplused. After a bit Jean asked Gwynne if he was going to the jail to pick up the boys.

"No...Just let them stew in their own juices," was his reply. After a while Jean again suggested he get the boys...Gwynne held fast and didn't budge.

"Gwynne...any bum who gets arrested, you go right to the jail to get them out, and here's your own flesh and blood in jail and you don't move...get up town and get them out of jail," Jean declared."

Not exactly a reunion, but a few of the principles in the Great Skunk Caper gather in 2007. From left to right, William Robbie Wallis, Sheriff William Kunkel, co-conspirator Todd Holden, and Blaine 'Buddy' Hans. Photo courtesy of the Holden Collection.

============

Coda

And so it was that the great prank was perpetrated. Once upon a time in a small town, you'll have boys who will be a tad bored by how things are on that particular evening and simply want to have a little fun. This is one time that caused a bit of a panic, but in the end was an evening well spent...especially 50-some years later.

Outhouses get planted on Main Street, soap bubbles pour out of water fountains, and quarters sometimes get nailed to the sidewalk while folks passing by try to pick up a little money. Then there's the infamous skunk deposit at the Bel Air Theater...another benchmark in the annals of deviant history.

============

This account of the incident in no way condones or advocates such behavior. Boys, if you're out there tonight having no fun and think of an idea that just might get you into trouble, maybe you should stay at home to try it...and even then, you might want to make sure one of your parents is an attorney.

========= 30 =========

STH

Canada Geese
'Lost and Found' Desk

From time to time folks pass little tidbits of information on to me and the current out-cropping of advices relates to the battle of landowners against 'resident' Canada geese...mind you, we all have no problems, at least I don't think there are any problems with migratory Canada geese.

It's the residents that are fed at local sediment ponds, then fly over to farm fields, like mine, to crap all over the embankments and in the water. The residents are used to being fed by 'do gooders' who live in the townhouses nearby, on Moore's Mill road and Southampton roads.

These geese are a nuisance in the biggest way. John Magness just finished harvesting this year's field corn crop and soon big gaggles of Canada geese will settle down for a night or two of feasting on the leftovers and then they'll be on their way south again. No problems with these guests.

The resident geese are another story. My pups, Frisco and Little Dude, are called into action with the flocks of 'residents' who fly in to the pond here at Rustica. I sic the pups on the birds, and soon they take flight, back over to Major's Choice, or wherever. I usually feed the bass and blue gill in the pond and often sit down by the pond to pass an afternoon. Having to traipse through geese muck just isn't my idea of relaxing, it's just a fact of

life when you have a fresh-water pond and the wildlife
that thrive in it and around it.

When I'm down by the pond, Frisco and Dude are
along for the adventure and the radars are up. If the
'residents' start to fly over while we're there, they divert
their flight and go somewhere else. Good friends Nan
and Billy Marshall also have a 'resident' problem on their
little spread on Glenville road. Nan said the mess left
by these geese is a real problem because she is usually
outside raking or tidying up the yard.

She doesn't have a dog like Frisco. Frisco's mom was
Bogey, a pure-bred Border Collie at Geneva Farm Golf
Course. It's in her blood to chase anything, and Bogey
as I'm told, was purchased by the golf course just for that
purpose, to chase geese off the fairways and greens.

Lots of golf courses use the same tactics to 'move'
the resident Canada geese away from otherwise pristine
areas. A private golf course superintendent told me
today the course management bought three dogs to be
used exclusively for patrolling the course and keeping
deer, fox and geese off the manicured parts of the course.
He said the dogs running have kept much of the problem
to an absolute minimum.

Well, now the old adage 'necessity is the mother
of invention'...comes into play. While Nan and I were
talking the other night, she pulled out an old harmonica
she had given one of her sons years ago, and it was left
behind when he moved on.

Nan Marshall serenades the geese. Photo by Todd Holden.

I urged her to play something on it, and she blew for a while and that was that.

The following day I received a call from Nan, excited as she told me of her experience that morning at her home. Seems a flock of Canada's settled in, near the pond at the house and she decided to take the harmonica and serenade the geese.

"You wouldn't have believed it Todd...they all heard me on the harmonica and sure enough, they took flight. They must not have liked the sound," she exclaimed. Said it suited her just fine. Imagine that, blowing a harmonica...I am not sure if Nan can actually 'play' anything yet...but the geese had to vamoose.

Thus it could be said, if you don't have a dog or a license to shoot Canada geese in season...you just might try a harmonica...heck, you might pick up a hobby playing it and enjoying the sound of your own music.

Known by friends as the *Stinkbug Whisperer,* for her prowess in communicating with stinkbugs, Nan's soulful serenading has expanded as she takes on the mantle of *Geese Whisperer.* Photo by Todd Holden.

***

On another note, this question from Betty Connor –

*"Good Afternoon Birdman. Hope you have a Happy
New Year.*

*"My question is this: for some reason all the finch left
our feeders last year, we had very few this summer. We
dumped the old seed, started with fresh and still no
finches come to feed. What is going on?*

*"Just thought you might have an answer to the
disappearance of the birds.*

"Have a good day."

*"Betty...the season has not been too harsh yet, so there
is an abundance of 'natural foods' for all the songbirds.
Sometimes they prefer to forage away from the feeders.
My advice is to re-fill the feeder with fresh black-
oil base sunflower seed, and just wait and see. Lots
of folks have not had the numbers of songbirds this
season, so far.*

All the best, Birdman."

========== 30 ==========

Airing Out The Stinkbug Thingy

The year of the stinkbugs...we all have been upset with these tough, slow-moving little insects. They are a nuisance for sure. Daughter, Mina Jean, had one fly into her eye, and she panicked as the stinkbug released the spray and for a couple of days the eye was quite painful.

Nothing bothered me more than earlier this year coming upstairs to bed and having 30 or so of them clinging and conjugating on the sliding glass door to the sunspace. Like many of you, I vacuumed them up; matter of fact, kept the little vacuum there in the bedroom since that was the area of most concern.

Around the house when Dude found one, he barked, and I would pick it up and either toss it down the sink drain or smash it with a napkin, whichever was closer.

Folks were buying stinkbug traps, trying to eliminate the pests. I was amazed they were so slow-moving and with practice got to the point they were easily picked up and carried outside and let loose.

Nan Marshall, alluded to in an earlier column, considers herself a 'stinkbug whisperer' and managed to keep things under control on Glenville Road most of the summer...sort of the 'live and let live syndrome'...which is fine.

The fall got under way this year and the stinkbugs wanted back inside. Now, I'm not sure how it was around your place, but those warm days in September brought about an invasion of sorts. This time it's a bit more clandestine...sneaky if you will. They seem to crawl on window screens looking for that little hole that got poked through some years back

My tee shirts hanging on the line sometimes have a stinkbug or two inside them. I hadn't noticed till I took one out of the closet to put on and felt something on my shoulder. It was a stinkbug and it gently flew to the carpet when I took the tee off.

Some have taken up residency in my Levelor blinds on the western windows. Others are creeping inside my truck, along the dashboard...and throughout this invasion I'm beginning to understand the stinkbugs a little more.

I'm not nearly as militant as I was earlier this year. Except for those onslaught days in September, they really don't bother me as much. Can't say that for the Dude though, he still doesn't like them and barks whenever he comes across one, which is a good thing. He's doing his job, earning his keep and being a pal and instinctively knows not to crush or eat them...smart dog.

STH

No doubt the most aggravating encounter with these bugs is when they are not seen on the floor and I come across one barefooted. That's a bummer, picking up the squashed mess, wiping up the floor and cleaning my foot. It's a small task I could do without.

Suffice to say though, it's not the end of the world. I haven't heard any of them talking and they don't seem to amass as though going into battle. They don't really sting, unless one 'squirts in your eye' as happened to Mina, and other than that they are just 'unwelcome guests' as Woody Guthrie once sang.

Today they were clinging to the tool shed door, and I let them be since nailing one with the fly swatter only makes a bigger mess on the door.

We all have our little pet peeves...Will Pardew can't stand ants in his home, but didn't mind a couple of 'white-footed mice' running around his shop in the winter time, getting close to the pot-bellied stove that usually was roaring to the delight of all visitors.

I'm not fond of mice in the house, or ants, or silverfish. I explained in a recent article my aversion to having crickets in the house, but don't really mind spiders and snakes. Go figure.

This morning, Dude spied one on the floor, letting me know with a couple of barks...I picked up the bug and tossed it outside in the fire pit. Better than wasting soapy water.

So, for now it seems, invasion of the stinkbugs isn't going to turn this world upside down. If they rise up on the Mayan calendar day when there will be locusts and frogs and all manner of calamity, a few extra stinkbugs won't matter. Except for the occasional, meandering stinkbug crawling on the wall or trying to find a quiet spot away from Dude, I think we can rest easy for the winter. The rite of passage will be in the spring when they all want to go back outside.

========= 30 =========

Scott Creek Takes Center Stage... Temporarily

A mid the enthusiasm I had believing articles I had written on behalf of Scott Creek, the Wye Trestle of the Ma and Pa railroad in Delta as well as the pristine beauty of Bunker Hill Road in Peach Bottom Township, suddenly this past Saturday it all seemed so helplessly forlorn. As I walked alone, I couldn't help but feel a sense of impending sadness, as though Mother Nature herself was dying.

The early morning rain left the dogwood, beech, oak and sycamore glistening with a bright shiny glow. There was no trash strewn about when I walked here as a kid, just water, trees, and trains. The scattered patch-work quilt of blue, white and green plastic jars, gallon containers and shopping bags stood out so terribly wrong in this otherwise tranquil scene of bygone days.

The landscape unfolded over the next little hill with more bags and sofas and recliners, tables, refrigerators, stereo cabinets...a veritable 'rummage sale' of unwanted household furnishings. These items once served a purpose and when worn out or replaced were destined for Scott Creek, a handy place to toss away what was not wanted.

I took a solitary walk south on the road made of soap-stone, slate and quartz...I wanted to walk the road before the slated cleanup began at 10 a.m.

STH

I had heard a property owner on the short road
wanted the right of way turned over to them and the
remainder of the roadway was to be closed forever. I
haven't been able to confirm that report, or meet with the
property owner...maybe soon that will be happen..

For now this absolutely pristine path to walk is a
picture perfect example of serenity...tranquility...all
the things a walking path should be are already there,
along with the rippling water soundtrack of Scott Creek,
peaceful and soothing as it meanders down the slope
from the roadway.

A pickup truck occupied by two men and a woman
passes by me heading north from Watson Road. They
each have somber faces as they settle in for their role in
the day's maneuvering of terrible litter to two huge roll-
off dumpsters.

The volunteers turned out in the misty morn and set
about the task of picking up as much litter as they could
from years of neglect and disrespect by folks using the
historic, short dirt road as a toxic waste dump under
cover of darkness.

An organization not even from this area, connected
with Keep York County Beautiful, spearheaded an effort
that included local volunteers and certainly made a dent
in restoring Scott Creek to more palatable conditions.
The conscientious effort by all those involved resulted in
filling a 40-yard and a 30-yard dumpster. A lot of debris
for a relatively small area.

One of many huge double-loads of all manner of debris and illegally dumped waste from a tri-state area is tended to during Saturday's massive clean up along Bunker Hill road. Photo by Todd Holden.

"We were looking for a large-scale cleanup site within a two-hour drive from Philadelphia. In 2010, Keep York County Beautiful did a survey of all the illegal dump sites in York County, and Bunker Hill Road was one of them," said Leslie Weinberg, of United By Blue, a Philadelphia-based, ocean-friendly apparel brand, which removes a pound of trash from oceans and waterways for every product sold.

In less than two years, they have removed 83,382 pounds from oceans and waterways in twelve states during 60 cleanups.

"For the past few months, I've been working with Tom Smith from Keep York County Beautiful to plan the logistics of the cleanup. We reached out to local press outlets to secure stories, volunteer groups to mobilize participants, mostly from the Delta area, local stores to donate breakfast, and the township to arrange trash removal," she noted.

The aura is undeniably reverent as the volunteers trudge up the first slope to begin their work. There is a surreal tranquility in this moment, as thoughts of days of youth, innocence, and adventure flood my mind. Days when Lane Hall and I walked the trestle before a southbound freight chugged into the Delta station.

As a kid I would walk the rails from the slaughter house, out and around the bend of the tracks to the ever-so-long wooden trestle as the line headed north to its final destination of York. In the distance was the long trestle I would try to walk across after a train crossed. It still looks as long as it did when I was a kid.

Moss has aged the wood...the rails long since taken up... a few large trees have fallen across parts of it, and still it stands, beautiful and strong and bold as ever. I remember slow moving freights at the station, loading or unloading, and I would race down Bunker Hill Road so I could get a good look as they crossed over the trestle.

Those days cannot be relived...only respected as part of the fabric of growing up and taking all of it for granted as we all did when we were younger. Time

A surrealistic scene indeed today, where once the famed Maryland and Pennsylvania railroad carried freight and passengers between York, Pennsylvania and Baltimore, Maryland...today, remnants of the Wye Trestle creates a scene of graceful beauty and memories of past glories. Photo by Todd Holden.

doesn't matter as much when you are younger, but as we grew it became a relentless wind that blew us into adulthood and away from this perfect preserve of nature. Sad gaps in days of youth and times past as we grew into other passages of our being.

Then, like finding an old pair of shoes that fit so well, we re-discover a place like Scott Creek and Bunker Hill Road, only to find the times have not been good to this natural beauty...she has been scarred by the relentless humans who come only to discard filth, junk, debris and toxic crap along her pristine embankments.

STH

I walk this same path today that I did as a kid sixty
years ago...it's the same road, same trestle, same creek...
but is it? All that I have hoped for in writing about
this parcel of Mother Nature's beauty is not to relive
my youth so much as to show respect for what is there.
Knowing this land growing up is my reference point,
my anchor; yet seeing the sea of plastic blue bags and
discarded junk strewn about, I am both sad and angry at
what has happened, what others have done.

Yet anger was something I felt before, when *'Massacre
At Scott Creek'* was written...in hopes that folks in the
area would pay attention to what they were doing and
reverse the slaughter. Now, a great sadness comes over
me as I wonder if enough has been done to alter the
course. Another two or three dumpsters could be filled
and a path could be built, but is it enough to make a
change? I am hoping my fellow Deltonians will see the
progress that has been made and take it from there. For
they surely must feel as attached to this land as I am.

The local volunteers who showed up today are
a blessing to the land...people who care. United By
Blue and Keep York County Beautiful are both to be
commended for the unheralded effort they have put
in. We each have a part and I hope that I have made a
difference as well. Mother Nature is a precious, spiritual
entity that we each have a hand in making timeless.

========= 30 =========

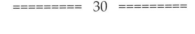

Sweet Corn and Cheap Hair Spray

It was New Year's Eve a couple of winter's ago and a first, when the potato gun was ignited for me. It exploded and sent a hefty spud hurtling into the open spaces over the crashing, cold Atlantic Ocean as it licked the filthy sands of Bethany Beach. Beyond spiritual, in a perverted kind of way; this was more of an awakening, but we'll get to that later on.

A few years ago I read about middle-aged professionals shooting tennis balls from crudely made contraptions using CO2 cartridges. I was never interested in launching tennis balls. But a hair spray-powered piece of plastic that can shoot a vegetable over 200 yards is another story.

Suffice it to say that on this historic New Year's Eve, one of our small party of holiday fun-seekers chose to honor the occasion by bringing forth this five-foot section of PVC, straight and true, with a 3-inch bore, full choke, and an impressive grip. I had no idea what was in store.

Threaded and capped on the business end with an igniter, the tightly stuffed potato is rammed into the chamber. It took two of us: one to spin the PVC cap into place after spraying AquaNet hairspray into the chamber, and another to aim and strike the igniter. The explosion was incredible. Loud and powerful. Cheap hairspray is best because it contains more alcohol, so they say.

My wife used to use AquaNet, and occasionally she doused me with it also, when we had to go out and look presentable. Seeing the red and white can, with the netting pattern on the logo sorta reminded me of her.

It was the potato that was the second revelation that chilly evening, preceding the festive falling ball of lights that descended from the pole in Times Square. Upon spewing forth, the potato launched into the night sky, going out of sight over the ocean. I couldn't believe what I'd just seen. Others in our small party were less baffled, by mere association with others who knew of this seemingly benign weapon.

A gentleman on the northwest side of Bel Air told me for less than $25 one could be made. "The key to making a good gun is to clean it thoroughly on the inside first, and use good glue. There's literally a bomb exploding inside this thing when it is ignited," he warned. "Not for children or those of feeble minds," another admonished.

Some might read this and say that I'm advocating violence. Then again, kids are killing other kids and teachers with real guns these days. Is there really a fine line between the potato gun and gun violence? Life is not easy these days, so what the heck, why not tell a story of the potato gun.

Sometimes life lets us know something funny and new, and when you tell someone else about it, they say they already know. I was brimming with excitement after that momentous New Year's Eve and later mentioned my activities to folks I ran into. Funny how many did not know of this 'gun.'

"I have Christmas orders already," one overly secretive manufacturer says. "I have already pulled up two web sites that deal with every aspect of 'Spud Guns' and 'Potato Boomers' so this isn't rocket science for the serious contender. In my case the mere behavior of folks with a potato gun is worth the watching," a mechanic from Aldino-Stepney says.

"You too can be the hit of a party. Bring a spud gun and a fifty-pound sack of taters and five or six cans of hairspray!" declares a young lady who sports a custom-made Spudzooka.

A few years ago at my 60th birthday party, a friend we'll just call Cannonball waited until late in the evening to unleash his gun. Three generations of family, friends and louts reveled in getting in line to launch potatoes high into the evening sky toward the pond, toward Hampton Ridge.

One slightly tipsy young lady fired one straight up into the overhang of my house. It was scary and funny at the same time. No one was hurt and no damage was done. Sometimes, you just have to let things fly.

STH

When the younger generation ran out of potatoes they tackled rolls, cheeses, apples, onions, sweet corn and even an expensive wedge of Brie. There was no time to run to the store.

In short, none of us could get enough of this new party game. No one walked away in disgust or indifference. There was gnashing of teeth when the last possible object was mustered for cannon fodder. The mood shifted from frivolity to bewilderment, as if the party was sitting inside the Alamo just when things really went bad for Sam Houston's troops.

A correspondent from the northern reaches of Harford County, who goes by the handle 'Crab Farmer' shares his enthusiasm when speaking of the performances by folks with all manner of backyard ballistics. "It's like a real cannon going off, and I've seen ears of sweet corn, tightly packed and shot out of sight. Just unbelievable, unbelievable," he notes.

The clandestine aspect of people with these creations lends credence to the suspected illegality of firing them, and sorta like cock fighting, no one speaks or advertises when a gathering may be graced by competitors vying for honors as if competing in the shot putt or javelin toss in the Olympics. Except, in the case of the potato gun, no animals are tortured. In fact, it's pretty safe as long as you stand on the back end of the explosion.

STH

That's the mystical nature of the potato gun.
Ingenuity and spontaneity always win out. We hear of
Volkswagen launchers, of pumpkin catapults, and of
potato guns. Men and women who want to shoot things
in the air and watch them go bye-bye.

Maybe all of this means nothing, sounding as an
empty, clanging cymbal in the night. Maybe no one
really cares whether or not he or she ever sees, or hears,
or better yet, fires a potato gun. Right! Things that
go bump in the night that you can't buy at Dick's or
Target, or at Sears Roebuck. There is no Ted Williams
Model Tater Launcher, for the comely price of $59.95 plus
shipping and handling. You gotta know somebody to get
a launcher. There has to be an invited guest to the party
who is the proud owner of the launcher.

In the night air, at the stroke of midnight on
December 31, 1999, when the big, tinsel ball fell
earthward, harkening in the New Year, it was the
orange and blue blast of hell-fire reflected in glassy eyes
marveling at such power and then seeing the potato,
the vegetable with all sort of baggage, belch forth like a
mortar round. Target or not, the hurtling missile crossed
the lines between sedation and life, between life and
death, between youthful hearts and stagnating, revelers
watching a stupid ball slide down a pole in Times
Square. America, apple pie, motherhood, spud gun.

Twelve years have passed since I was first introduced to the potato gun. I tried shooting the rude, local geese, but couldn't find anyone to help me screw on the lid when I needed the help. To tell you the truth, I haven't been inside a grocery store to look for AquaNet, although I'm sure there's a can on the shelf. So, I'm older, yet wiser for the experiences I have had with this most home grown of grown up pieces of entertainment. We aimed for the sky and somewhere, there's a potato still in orbit.

========= 30 =========

Disclaimer: Interestingly enough, the Bureau of Alcohol Tobacco and Firearms doesn't consider spud guns a threat to the sanctity of human life, or the American way. Like everything, common sense and good judgment will always win out.

Thoughts On Owning A Gun

When I was a kid, my dad let it be known that he didn't like bullets...not to mention guns. Seems when he was a kid in Delta delivering papers, he was standing by a barrel that had a fire in it for the delivery boys to keep warm on a winter's morning. As a joke, one of the boys tossed a couple bullets into the barrel and they went off, blowing a hole in the side of the rusty barrel.

Had a negative effect on my dad and he told me the story when I was very small. To my knowledge he never owned a gun. His father did, Ches Holden, a constable in Delta, had shotguns, rifles and a couple of pistols. Ches hunted every season with his beagles. He brought home food for the table at his home on Park Avenue behind the brick telephone exchange.

He kept the beagles out back in a kennel, next to the garage and the wood shop. I never went hunting with him when the seasons came in for rabbit, squirrel and deer. Although I was curious, I was too little to go hunting and then I lost my grandfather. Ches died of a heart attack sitting in his chair by the window, waiting for Grandma Addie to come home from her 10 p.m. to 7 a.m. shift as a telephone operator when I was only 10 years old.

STH

About the same time my family moved to
Southampton Farm, a sprawling 550-acre dairy farm near
Bel Air. Every kid who worked on the farm had a 22
rifle to shoot groundhogs with. They shot groundhogs
whenever there was time and their dads bought them
ammo at the Fountain Green stores, Carrico's and
Stamper's. Groundhogs and the holes they dug were
a big nuisance to the farmers operating tractors and
machinery in the fields of hay and corn.

I asked my Dad if I could have a rifle, he said 'no' in
no uncertain terms. So my mom and I went to Carrico's
one day and Joe Carrico sold her a single-shot Remington
22. He even tossed in a box of ammo in the deal. Mom
used to shoot when she lived in Manitou Springs,
Colorado. So she took me to the meadow behind the
house to shoot tin cans. We had such fun.

Until Dad came home one day and spotted us. He
made us take the rifle back to Mr. Carrico. Joe came to
defend us, saying, 'Gwynne, the boy lives on a farm,
there's plenty of groundhogs to shoot, and he wants to
do what the other boys are doing. Besides, the farmers
don't like groundhogs and the damage they do.'

Reluctantly, Dad let me keep the rifle with certain
restrictions. Again he related the story of the bullets in
the fiery barrel back in Delta so many years before. I
couldn't hold it against dad for being so stubborn about
guns, and his story always did stick in the back of my

mind. The restrictions he put on me helped me learn how to respect owning a gun too; so Dad did the right thing.

Soon I became a pretty good shot, and would bring home one and sometimes two groundhogs. In the spring they were fried up and considered a delicacy by my mom's helper, Martha "Dolly" Hammond. I can still remember her making me her homemade brownies when I would bring in a fresh killed 'hog.'

My brother Brian was lucky, because my trials with Dad made it a little easier for him to get into hunting with me. Then Brian took it to another level, deer hunting in Western Maryland, with some friends I had met while at the University of Maryland, College Park.

First day out, Brian got his buck, one shot, clean kill, and he wanted to come home with his prize. The landowner dressed the deer out and we tied it across the trunk of that white Falcon Futura and headed home. He kept the buck on the car while we stopped at Richardson's in Bel Air for everyone to admire.

The photo with this story of the way old time hunters tied their 'kill' over their shoulder reminded me of Brian and me hauling the buck back to the camp that cold day in 1963.

STH

Bringing in the kill, old-time style. Not quite the same today.
Hunting Deer. A deer hunt near Deadwood, Winter '87-'88. Two
miners, McMillan and Hubbard, got their game. Photo by John C. H.
Grabill.

So it goes today, I still hunt groundhogs living here at
Rustica...I have been invited to target shoot with a good
friend at a range up near the Buck across the river, but
so far haven't been enthused about it. I only shoot when
there's a varmint or 'problem intruder'...let's just leave it
at that.

I do not collect guns. I believe we all have the right
to own and use a gun because ownership doesn't make
us criminals intent on hurting someone or committing
a crime. Bad folks are out there, for sure, but that's just
it, it's the criminal not the gun. Thus, if this 'gun take
away' ever comes to be...who do you honestly think

STH

will turn over the guns...the law abiding folks likely...
certainly not the criminals who didn't get permits and
buy the guns legally.

What my Dad taught me has stayed with me. The
fellas who threw the bullets in the barrel probably
went on to more criminal things...maybe not, hope
not. But the truth about owning a gun is a peaceful
intervention...Joe Carrico did me a great service and all
the lessons I learned along the way taught me how to
respect a gun.

Taking away the right to own a gun is plain wrong,
just sayin'.

========= 30 =========

Too Little Acclaim Given To Late Songwriter Fields Ward

Very seldom do we know or get to meet someone who has so much talent to be able to write and play his own music, and then, in a whisper, to see them gone without ever receiving the recognition they deserved. Such is the story of Fields Ward, whose daddy, Davey Crockett Ward, wrote the following observation on his 80th birthday....

"This is no song, but plain truth. Most old people don't have much fun in life. The greater part of their work is done and many of them grieve because they feel they are not needed anymore. Do you contribute to the happiness of those you know? Or do you deal them little deadly wounds? Are you sharp and impatient with them when they don't hear what you said, or do you just repeat it quietly?"

"Do you take a few minutes to stop and talk to them or are you too busy to take the time? When they express opinions of modern trend, are you one of those who says old fogey ideas, or do you listen to what they say? When they try to do a little work, do you try to make them feel like they had been a great help, or do you make them feel like they are in the way?"

STH

"If you live you will be eighty someday yourself. How would you like for young folks to treat you when that day comes?" Written by Crockett Ward at 2 o'clock P.M. March 19, 1943.

Into this environment, Fields Ward was born on January 23, 1911 on Buck Mountain, a half a dozen miles west of Independence, VA. His father and mother made music together, him fiddling and her singing, and in time the children picked up guitar and banjos and joined in. This was mainly wintertime entertainment "homegrown style" and it was a way of passing along the folklore of the land from generation to generation.

Crockett kept little notebooks filled with poetry and songs he heard and made up. From one of the notebooks, I came across a poem called "The Dying Hobo." It reads, "I'm going to a better land where everything is bright. Where hand-outs grow on bushes and you can sleep out every night. And you never have to work at all and never change your socks. And little streams of whiskey come trickling down the rocks."

In the margin of the old, yellowed tablet where I found this poem, Crockett had noted in ink, "Could be good." I should say so; the entire poem is one of the best I've ever read. Pure and simple, direct and honest and written by someone who had a definite feeling for the subject—the life of a hobo.

Today in the Ward kitchen, Fields' widow, Naomi, remembers the good her husband did in helping alcoholics who were down and out. He touched many lives after having taken "the cure" himself at Keswick Grove, New Jersey, many years ago. Fields was in the program three months and came home a new man.

I only wish he had received the recognition he deserved for the music he made. It was part of a large group of material recorded live and now in the Library of Congress. Fields died October 26, 1987, and in his folders are letters from agents and people who said they could help him with publishing and making a name for himself, but he became disillusioned with the fast talk and the empty promises.

Back in 1939 a fellow named Alan Lomax came to Roanoke to record folk songs. He was with the Archive of American Folk Song and the Library of Congress. The local station, WDBJ, did a program for the American School of the Air, that sent Fields, his father and three other musicians known as the Bog Trotters, all across the nation, coast to coast, live and into the homes and schools of an appreciative audience. The program, one of a series, won the top award, first place, for Educational Radio Programming that year. It looked like Fields, the youngest member of the group, was on his way.

The Bog Trotters music was from Scotland, Ireland and England, and with the tapping of feet, strumming of banjos and guitars, these five mountain men passed on stories from the Southwest Virginia mountains. Fields recorded and sold his music, sometimes earning a penny or a nickel for his effort and talent.

His battles included alcohol, agents and pirating performers who ripped off his music that was supposed to be sacred in the hallowed halls of the Library of Congress. Parents of folksingers and so-called friends of Fields Ward and his wife, Naomi, figure prominently in the loss and lack of credit for much of his original music. In this scenario of similar songs and unanswered questions, there are many more devils and demons, of alcohol and worthless papers, contracts and agreements.

One song in particular, "Train On The Island," written by Fields and recorded with his label, Coal Creek Music, Inc., was copyrighted and supposed to earn him a penny for each record sold. A variation of the song, according to Fields, turned up being performed by the New Lost City Ramblers.

In his folder, the last letters from the Library to Fields were left unanswered. Fields was filled with disillusionment and bitterness and distrust, things that never entered his mind in the creative years.

The scrapbooks are filled with the joy and enthusiasm of the development of a creative force that was self-taught and with an endless source of material....there are blue ribbons from Fiddlers Conventions in Galax and the

song sheet from the big radio broadcast...8 little songs that made a difference as to how the nation heard folk music in its pre form, live and honest.

Fields worked as a farm hand, and then as a housepainter until failing health forced him to retire. His legacy is a passel of songs, melodies, recordings, and memories. His undeniable genius, to those who knew and loved him, has not gone unnoticed. Their only wish is that the songs were published and recorded on a scale afforded to other musicians with less talent and ability.

But this story is not unique, it happens to many of those we know. It's just that when you listen to the words, you realize the message was true and you wish that others could have heard it too.

"Yonder comes my old true love, how do you reckon I know. I know her by her apron string tied in a double bow." From "Train On The Island" by Fields Ward...

Fields last sang in public in a concert in New York in 1983. He performed with Paul Brown, and he sold a box of his records. The two-hour concert filled him with joy and relief. Four years later this gifted songwriter was dead, but his contributions to country music, especially folklore and folk music, will go on forever.

Mrs. Ward said her favorite song was one she and Fields sang together, "Three Leaves of Shamrock," written by James McQuine in 1889.

Today, from her modest home in Bel Air, Naomi sits
with her devoted family and friends, and her precious
memories of a man who created music from the heart,
and conquered a demon that we all fear. Sitting in one of
the rooms is the beautiful, dark guitar that her husband
played....there is a magic about it, and what it represents
to anyone who has ever seen the peaks and dreaded the
valleys.

"The last time one of those fellows from the city
came up here and tried to get Fields to give him a song,
he just put his foot down and said, 'No, that's it, no
more.' I knew he had just had enough," Mrs. Ward said.
"Besides, we all know his music speaks for itself...it was
his work with alcoholics that means so much to us, to
those whose lives Fields touched and healed. That is a
lasting memory too, and no one can ever take that away
from him."

========= 30 =========

Now He Sits In Her Chair

Recently, two men I know lost the loves of their life, the women they were married to for many years. Both men were devoted husbands, both suffered a loss that no man can repair.

In most families, the women generally outlive the men, sometimes by quite a few years. More frequently it seems it is the husbands who are surviving the wives. No less painful for the survivor, still, for the husband to outlive the wife the void seems the bigger grief to bear.

For the two gentlemen I speak of, the marriages were a beautiful courtship for as long as they were together. As the couples grew older they grew closer to one another. The couples were Dr. Drex Johnston and his wife, Imogene, and Bud Hans and his wife, Deloris 'Johnnie' Hans. Mrs. Hans is survived by her husband of 38 years, Blaine 'Buddy' Hans of Forest Hill, Maryland.

I was asked to deliver the eulogy for Imogene, a prominent politician in these parts and a most gracious lady. I wrote about her in an earlier column in The Star. Johnnie Hans was 90 years old when she passed away, after breaking her hip and being hospitalized. During her lifetime she was known to many through her job as Court Commissioner for the State of Maryland and Harford County before retiring. She was also a member of Grandview Christian Church in Fallston, Maryland.

STH

Bud Hans was a policeman most of his life and before that delivered newspapers. He and I go way back to when I was a kid of 15 and Bud was a town policeman in Bel Air.

At his wife's funeral services Bud mentioned to me how much he and Johnnie were in love, and how special that was. It is truly special to reach old age with the one you fell in love with a long time ago.

His family told me at the funeral services how they liked the story I had done on Bud and that they had read the story out loud as they gathered at home in these past few days. I had to be honest and let them know I did not recall ever writing a story about Bud. "Sure you did," they told me. "All about that time you let the skunk loose in the Bel Air Theater and Dad had to arrest you." Then I remembered. Yet, I only mention this because the family told me it had meant so much for them to read the story together and laugh and share a moment during this time of grief.

To tell the truth, Bud didn't really want to arrest me that night. He just looked at what I did as a harmless joke by a 15-year old kid.

Bud has not been in the best of health himself, but actually looked pretty good at the funeral home and services. He has some tough days ahead and family and friends will play a big role in that period of adjustment.

STH

One thing he said to me struck a note that I'd never thought about before. I thought how striking and poignant his sentiments were.

He said he now sits in 'Johnnie's chair in the living room,' not his own chair anymore.

"Sitting in her chair keeps me calm, because I'm not sitting in my own chair, looking over to where she used to sit. I'm not looking at her empty chair and feeling bad, Todd. I'm looking at my own, empty chair, and that's not so bad," he said. The words came from his heart and they certainly touched mine.

Never thought of that as a way of dealing with loss. I don't think I'll ever be able to sit in a living room chair without thinking of all of my loved ones who are not with me. Kind of a spiritual way to look at things I suppose.

I've also spoken with Drex Johnston since his wife's passing. He has moments he said where he just wants to lie down and reflect on the life they shared so many years. He loved her very much and I am sure he will hold on to that love just as though Imogene were sitting with him. Love does transcend quite a few things.

It's understandable to grieve in different ways, as any of us know full well; we just do what we have to do to keep moving and functioning. Sometimes things overwhelm us when it comes to the loss of a loved one.

Each of us has to find the ways to continue on when the person in our life is taken away, and it doesn't get any easier as the years roll by. Family and friends provide a lot of support to get through the rough spots, but the void just can't be filled.

What these two men are doing though is about as honorable as it gets. As hard as it is, both are honoring and remembering their cherished ones with the same strength of love they had when their spouses were alive. In that regard, the vows hold up long after death do us part.

========= 30 =========

As Long As...

S omeone asked me the other day what I was doing now that I'm retired from studio days on Pennsylvania Avenue in Bel Air. It's hard for me to say 'I'm not doing anything'...so I don't say that, because it's not true. I'm busy with photo archiving and still writing and trying to put a book together of the very best columns written.

So when someone asks that question it gives me pause and usually I say that I still tend the land here at Rustica, still enjoy mowing with the old International diesel tractor and still enjoy pruning and planting shrubbery.

Of course I have my pals, Dude, Chester and Frisco to share time with. Some little health setbacks and still on the right side of the dirt. I'm quite lucky to be alive and count my blessings, which takes a good while some days.

To tell the truth I don't sit in front of the television all day doing nothing. I rise early in the day, and usually am busy until bedtime depending on the weather. If I don't have anything planned and written on the calendar, I generally stay busy creating adventures.

So, again it happened the other day running into an old acquaintance who asked what I was doing these days. When I got home the following notes just poured out....

STH

As long as...

As long as there's a tear in my eye for a friend's passing on...

As long as there's pain shared when a friend is hurting...

As long as there's a smile from within my heart...

As long as there's a puppy that runs to get my attention...

As long as there's a woman's touch on my cheek...

As long as there's a sunrise bringing visions of the day ahead...

As long as there's appreciation for sharing the goodness of ideas...

As long as I live...I'll write...to share what I think is worthy

As long as others might enjoy and relate to what I write...that's for them to decide.

My thoughts, ideas, decisions come from within a place, of mystery, of magic, of doubt and fear...

As long as they keep coming...I must write.

The author, right, stands with his long standing friend and fellow journalist, the late Duane Henry. Photo by Keith Holbrook.

So as long as I'm able, it's the writing that will continue...just the way it is.

========= 30 =========

Made in the USA
Middletown, DE
20 September 2016